EDWIN P. HOYT served in the U.S. Army
Air Corps and in the Office of War Informa-
tion before he became a war correspondent
for United Press International. He also
worked for both the *Denver Post* and the
American Broadcasting Company in the Far
East, Europe, and the Middle East in the
years following World War II. Hoyt is the
author of many military history books, in-
cluding *The Men of the Gambier Bay*,
McCampbell's Heroes, *Bowfin*, *The Sea
Wolves*, and *The Carrier War*, as well as the
War in the Central Pacific series: *Storm
Over the Gilberts*, *To the Marianas*, and
Closing the Circle.

LEYTE GULF

—GULF—

THE DEATH OF THE PRINCETON

—EDWIN P. HOYT—

AVON
PUBLISHERS OF BARD, CAMELOT, DISCUS AND FLARE BOOKS

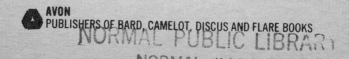

All photographs in the insert are courtesy of the National Archives.

AVON BOOKS
A division of
The Hearst Corporation
105 Madison Avenue
New York, New York 10016

Copyright © 1972 by Edwin P. Hoyt
Published by arrangement with the author
Library of Congress Catalog Card Number: 87-91210
ISBN: 0-380-75408-8

First Avon Printing: October 1987

AVON TRADEMARK REG. U.S. PAT. OFF. AND IN OTHER COUNTRIES, MARCA
REGISTRADA, HECHO EN U.S.A.

Printed in the U.S.A.

K–R   10   9   8   7   6   5   4   3   2   1

CONTENTS

CHAPTER ONE

Life

When, at the end of December, 1941, Admiral Chester W. Nimitz arrived at Pearl Harbor to assume command of the Pacific Fleet of the United States Navy, he found a fleet whose whole method of action must be changed. In an earlier time the fleet had depended on its battleships and cruisers as a first line of defense. But the battleships lay crippled or dead in the water of Pearl Harbor, or had been dispatched already to the West Coast's shipyards for major repairs.

To fight the war in the Pacific, then, Admirals Ernest J. King and Chester W. Nimitz felt they must depend upon an entirely new strategy; they had to forego the use of battleships because they could not put the battleships to sea. And, indeed, by the time the old battleships were repaired and the force augmented from the other side of the world, naval strategy had so changed that they were never employed at all in the manner that the great strategists of the past had dreamed.

The Japanese attack on Pearl Harbor taught the world that there would be a new kind of naval warfare in the middle of the twentieth century. The new fleet warfare would depend on aircraft carriers, developed in the First World War by aviators and forward looking seamen, but

1

scoffed at by the ''battleship admirals'' as too fragile a weapon to bear major responsibility in action.

All the old reasoning suddenly meant nothing when America found herself without battleships, and with only a handful of aircraft carriers, cruisers, and destroyers for a fleet. Of course there were submarines, but their purpose was to fight lonely battles, to search out the enemy's shipping vessels and destroy them, and to sink his fighting ships if they could. The fleet war, if there was to be one, would have to depend on a new concept, and the strong weapon here was the aircraft carrier.

The change in the method of naval warfare brought about some vital changes in the thinking of America's admirals. The physical evidence soon began to show, and one manifestation of it was to be found in the regular meetings between Admiral Chester Nimitz and Admiral Ernest J. King. The latter was Chief of Naval Operations and an aviation-minded admiral, but Admiral Nimitz had not been so in the beginning. Yet he was so brilliant a commander that in a short time he had trained himself to think along aviation lines—and the war effort in the Pacific gained from his training.

Since the beginning of the war, Admirals King and Nimitz would bring their key staff members together every few months; usually at San Francisco, to discuss the problems and progress of the war. From those earliest meetings and from King's brilliant leadership, came the conversion of nine ships, which were to play vital roles in the war against the Axis powers.

In 1941, when war was brewing in the Pacific and raging in Europe, an aroused Congress had supported the drastic strengthening of the navy, and out of this support came commissions for nine cruiser hulls which were laid down in various naval yards. One of these, laid on June 2, 1941, was to become the carrier *Princeton*—or CVL-23, which means Light Carrier No. 23.

The keel of this ship was laid at the New York Shipbuilding Corporation in Camden, New Jersey, and the building went on with the slow-steadiness that marked naval shipbuilding before the Second World War. But when the electrifying news of the bombing of Pearl Harbor came, the Bureau of Ships began to take stock, and out of it came the conversion plans. The *Princeton* was launched at an impressive ceremony on October 18, 1942, and the champagne was broken across her bow by Mrs. Harold Dodds, wife of the President of Princeton University. She was the fourth ship of the navy to bear the name; others had been the first screw-propelled ship of the navy, a second, bigger ship, and a gunboat, in service from 1895 to 1919.

Princeton was commissioned on February 25, 1943, and after a shakedown cruise she departed for the Pacific under Captain George R. Henderson. Her coming, along with that of ships like her, and those of the bigger fleet carrier classes was to completely change the war in the Pacific. Where before a task force was built about one or two carriers, by this time Admiral Nimitz and his subordinates were thinking in grander terms. After the tremendous victory at the Battle of Midway in the summer of 1942, Vice Admiral Raymond Spruance was put to work forming the Fifth Fleet. Its essence: a huge task force of carriers, new fast battleships, cruisers, destroyers, and all the ships that must supply such a fleet.

As the Americans moved north from Australia and east into the Pacific, they sought bases and one of these was Baker Island, which was attacked on September 1. *Princeton* was one of the leaders in this attack, and one of the new carriers provided with F6F Hellcat fighter planes, to replace the old F4Fs, developed as a result of the Japanese successes with the Zero. By this time *Princeton*'s pilots, led by Lt. Comdr. Henry L. Miller, were ready. They had spent months practicing carrier landings and takeoffs, and perfecting their flight patterns and their shooting eyes.

There was some trouble that first day of operations—the kind that a captain might face at any time. Here, going into their maiden action, the catapult broke down, creating confusion and difficulty in launching the heavy torpedo planes. The fighters had the glory this trip. Most of it went to Lt. (jg) R.L. Loesch and Ensign A.W. Nyquist, who flew out over Howland Island looking for Japanese planes, in support of the troops landing on Baker Island. They were vectored out at 10,000 feet to meet a bogey—a pip on the radar screen. As the two pilots came in, flying their new fast planes, they found that the "bogey" was an "Emily," a four-engined Japanese bomber, with a camouflage paint of green and brown, and wearing the rising Sun insigniate on its wingtips and tail. That tail wore something else, too—a machine gun protruding from a turret.

The two F6Fs swooped down from 10,000 feet on the unsuspecting bomber, three thousand feet below them, just as the Emily turned half around on her mission—whatever it might have been. The two American pilots came down out of the sun, Loesch first and then Nyquist, running from overhead, and firing as soon as they got within five hundred yards of the enemy.

The first attack struck home, and after the second, the Japanese bomber turned her right wing down, and fell into an easy right spiral, streaming gasoline as she fell. She hit the water hard, so hard that a geyser spouted up 1000 feet, the pilots said. They circled, and watched, for it was their first kill and the first of their proud carrier. No Japanese crewmen came to the surface.

Two days later, on the heels of quiet, the pilots of Fighter Squadron 23 got under Emily—big bomber—just off Baker Island. There were four pilots involved this time, Lt. (jg) H.G. Odenbrett, Ensign A.R. Roberts, Lt. (jg) T.T. Coleman and Ensign E.J. Philippe. They were flying to intercept any Japanese planes that tried to interfere with the landing operations on Baker Island, and six miles ahead of them, at 7,000 feet they saw another Emily just after one o'clock in the afternoon. It was a tougher problem this day than it had been before, because the sky was cloudy, half filled with large, high cumulus clouds—an excellent hiding place for an airplane.

The Japanese saw them this time, and started a tight flipper turn of 160 degrees into a cumulus cloud. Odenbrett went after the plane, trying a flat tail run, but it was not effective. Roberts made a steep high-side run, trying to kill some of the Emily crew, but then the bomber was gone into the cloud. To find her, Coleman and Philippe circled around and close to the left—and sure enough—out of the bottom of the cloud, dropping all the time, came the bomber. Coleman and Philippe jettisoned their auxiliary gas tanks to gain more speed and set off in pursuit. The Japanese hopped from one cloud to another, trying desperately to escape the faster fighter planes. Coleman caught the plane though, with three tail runs. Gasoline began streaming from the tank near the outboard port engine of the Japanese plane. Philippe then caught up, and opened fire from 600 yards out, scoring hits that he could see. The Japanese pilot tried to escape by dropping down to wave level, then he lost control, and the plane hit the water, exploding as it hit. The Americans made more runs, strafing debris in the water, which appeared to them to be heads of the Japanese crew.

They went back to the carrier, undamaged. There was a little more excitement five days later when pilots from the *Princeton* got another of the patrol bombers, but that was all. It was an indication of the changing fortunes of war, even in 1943, that the landings on Baker Island were so quiet. The Japanese fleet was licking wounds suffered in the battles of Guadalcanal, and it would be many months before the fleet would come out again to oppose the Americans.

And yet there would be tragedies for the men of *Princeton*, for this was war and it was always uncertain what might happen on a mission over the sea. The Japanese were the enemy, to be sure, but so could be the weather, and the sea itself, as they all were on September 18, 1943, when *Princeton*'s airmen, along with those of *Lexington* and

Belleau Wood carried out a softening-up raid on Makin and Tarawa atolls.

The big target that day was Tarawa, which was the object of *Princeton*'s second strike of the day. It was still dark when the planes took off, and the blackness and clouds made it hard for the pilots to keep formation as they flew the 90 miles from ship to target. The torpedo bombers were armed that day with five-hundred pound bombs, very effective against shipping and shore installations, and they flew in at a low altitude to Tarawa and then climbed to as high as 7,000 feet as they came in about 15 miles away from target. They came in across Buota Island in the atoll of Tarawa, and then approached their targets on Bititu Island. While the fighters that accompanied the planes circled overhead and strafed the ground installations, the bombers made their runs. Their targets were planes on the ground (or in the air if they found any) and the anti-aircraft positions around the airfields on the islands. They also wanted to hit buildings, ammunition dumps, and anti-aircraft positions elsewhere on the island, and if possible to knock out the Japanese gasoline storage system.

Planes from the three carriers swarmed around the target, meeting virtually no air resistance, although the anti-aircraft fire was sometimes fierce. There was some minor damage to planes—until the fifth strike. Then matters grew more serious. Eight *Princeton* TBFs took off on that strike, at 8:50 in the morning. *Princeton* was holding her position, about ninety miles off the island, but the pilots of this strike were slow in arriving at the target because they had difficulty in keeping together. They came in at just about ten o'clock in the morning, which meant the Japanese had good visibility from the ground. All went well with the first runs, but when Lt. (jg) C.M. Bransfield came in for his run, the anti-aircraft fire became deadly, and he was taking hits. He pulled out from a glide dive at the target, near the south end of a pier, and other planes saw black smoke trailing from his engine. He pulled out at 1,500 feet and moved across the island, followed by others who watched anxiously as he headed south, gradually losing altitude. Then, about four miles south of Bititu Island, the lieutenant force landed into the water. She splashed, and stayed afloat for about forty seconds. Other pilots flying over saw Bransfield and his crew in their rubber boat, waving to them. They reported the position, but then they had to go on back to the carrier, with the presumption that their friends would be rescued not by them but much more likely by the enemy.

It was a tough war, and *Princeton* was in the middle of it, as a carrier of the fast carrier task force that alternated under the command of Admiral Spruance (Fifth Fleet) and Admiral William F. Halsey (Third Fleet). Actually most of the ships and many of the air groups were the same, no matter which admiral was in charge. And this year, 1943, they were busy softening up the Japanese for coming Central Pacific invasions.

Princeton had her troubles. In November, 1943, she was seized by an attack of excessive vibrations, which seemed to increase and prevented her from maintaining peak performance. Indeed, the captain was worried lest some serious engineering difficulties arise. What would happen if she were to break down at sea? True, the Japanese submarine service was not as effective as it might be, but what a tempting target a stopped carrier would make— anytime, any place. The vibrations grew worse, and soon the ship was having trouble with her steering, so with some unhappiness, she was detached at the end of the Gilbert Islands occupation, and sent back to Pearl Harbor for repairs. With her she took station near the other carriers, and sent off her operational planes, for the most part, and took on their damaged planes. On December 1, as she made ready to steam back to Pearl, she had all her pilots of Air Group 23—who stayed with the ship. But as far as planes were concerned, she had only three torpedo planes and six fighters, plus one wrecked fighter, just enough planes to manage anti-submarine patrol on the way home to Hawaii.

At Pearl, *Princeton* went into drydock, and the cause of the vibrations was eliminated. In January, 1944, she was ready to take part in the occupation of the Marshalls, and to play her role as a fighting ship in that important battle.

On January 30, *Princeton* struck Wotje Island as a part of the task force, smashing radio stations, radar installations, planes, and shipping in the atoll. D-Day was January 31 for occupation of Kwajalein and Majuro atolls, and *Princeton* was in action near Wotje. Here, in the laconic style of the professional navy, is the report of what the carriers did that day, taken from *Princeton*'s war diary:

"At 0624 USS *Saratoga* commenced launching aircraft. Maneuvered throughout the day to maintain a position generally 75 miles distant from both Wotje and Taroa Islands, running downwind, approximately, between flight operations, and zig-zagging in accordance with Plan 9 when not conducting flight operations. At 0719 completed launching four VF [fighters] for combat air patrol . . . and eight VF and five VT [bombers] for strike . . . on Wotje Island.

"At 0815 received an order from OTC [officer in tactical command] directing that a report be made upon the condition of the runways and the general situation of Wotje Island upon the return of the first strike.

"At 0906 completed launching three VT and four VF for Combat Air Patrol No. 2AA over Wotje Island.

"At 0937 completed recovery of Strike No. 1A. Results of Strike No. 1A were as follows:

"Five VT (bombers) dropped three 1000-pound bombs near radio station and two 2000-pound bombs which hit the shop area, reporting that the radio building was concrete and strafing was ineffective; three radio towers still standing. Eight VF made several strafing runs on buildings. Moderate light anti-aircraft fire was observed from the southeast shore. Runways were well-pitted, the ammunition dump fire (set the day before) was still burning, and many barracks were burned out. All planes returned; one VT received minor damage from an explosive shell.

"At 1004 received order from OTC to return USS *Saratoga* TBM 1C with pilot and crew to USS *Saratoga* at 1130. [This plane had landed on *Princeton* in an emergency, as was not uncommon among the carriers.]

"At 1040 sighted USS *Chester* and two destroyers bearing 125 degree distance six miles.

"At 1130 completed launching four VF and four VT for strike No. 3A on Wotje Island and four VF for Combat Air Patrol No. 3AA.

"At 1131 received order from OTC to place all future bombs on the runway at Wotje Island, using no long delay fuses. At 1140 completed recovering strike No. 2A and Combat Air Patrol No. 2AA. Results of strike No. 2A were as follows: 2 VT dropped 24 100-pound bombs in ammunition dump area, third VT was returned to the USS *Saratoga*, results not received. Eight VF of Combat Air Patrol 1AA strafed the radio station, buildings, boats, and an island four miles northeast of Wotje. Most buildings reported gutted. Nineteen various small boats on the lagoon shore are all sunk or holed. Five ammunition dumps are still standing, three are burning or burned. The dock crane and seaplane ramp are undamaged. All planes returned, one VT to the USS *Saratoga*. Two planes received minor damage from small caliber anti-aircraft fire [the Japanese usually used 25 AA guns].

"At 1237 received order from OTC to install belly tanks for remaining Combat Air Patrols this date [to give longer air time.]

"At 1245 completed launching four VF for Combat Air Patrol over Wotje Island.

"At 1305 Lieutenant (jg) S.G. Bucklew in F6F No. 15 was hit over the target and injured. His plane headed toward the ship and was seen to make a hard, forced landing 15 miles, bearing 095 degrees from Wotje Island. Several VT from this vessel circled an oil slick after seeing the crash, but found no trace of pilot after 20-minute search.

"At 1308 observed plane crash in walkway aboard USS *Langley* [another carrier nearby].

"At 1315 OTC ordered previously contemplated fuelling of destroyers from cruisers this date cancelled.

"At 1324 VF-4 in landing, accidentally discharged 300 rounds of .50 caliber into the flight deck; no casualties resulted from gun fire but three men were injured seeking cover.

"At 1327 received order from OTC directing Combat Air Patrol No. 5C to cover the USS *Preble* searching to the westward of Maloelap Atoll for a lost pilot from the USS *Enterprise*, returning on schedule.

"At 1332 completed recovery of Combat Air Patrol 2AA and Combat Air Patrol 3AA and strike No. 3A. Results of strike were as follows: Four VT dropped one 2,000-pound bomb near the runway, eight 500-pound bombs on the runway, and four 500-pound bombs in the fuel storage area. Four VF dropped four 500-pound bombs on the runways. [This was the first actual use of VF fighters, to carry bombs from this vessel, except in practice, where they had carried one 1,000-waterfilled bombs each.] Twelve VF, including two combat patrols, made numerous strafing runs. Fires were reported started in the fuel pumps and several buildings were burned to the ground. Two previously reported ammunition dump fires were still burning as were many other small fires. Rows of fuel drums on an island four miles northeast of Wotje were all burned out. One VF lost [as reported at 1305 above]. Six VF received slight damage from small calibre anti-aircraft fire.

"At 1400 the fleet axis was rotated to the left to 060 degrees, more closely corresponding with the latest prevailing winds. [This was a decision of Admiral Mitscher's of course, as Officer in Tactical Command. It was his responsibility to keep his carriers operating as a fleet, and the wind made a great deal of difference, since a carrier almost had to launch and recover planes while facing into the wind. As can be seen by the *Princeton*'s war diary of this one day, the key to American carrier operation was teamwork and fleet control—as in this case *Princeton*'s men felt an almost personal responsibility to see that Wotje's air defenses were knocked out and the way was paved for the landing forces to move with a minimum of opposition.]

"At 1542 completed catapulting four VT [torpedo bombers] for A/S [anti-submarine] patrol.

"At 1543 sighted a US Navy PB4Y search plane five miles ahead of formation.

"At 1547 completed launching four VF for Combat Air Patrol 5C over Taroa Island and Combat Air Patrol 5AA over Wotje Island.

"At 1557 completed recovery of Combat Air Patrol No. 4AA.

"At 1616 received order from OTC to drop photographs of Wotje Island on each cruiser concerned tomorrow, and to drop on the USS *Saratoga* the latest pictures of both targets. [The reason was that the cruisers would bombard the island the next day, and the photographs would give them an idea of the best targets, while the commander of the force, in *Saratoga*, wanted a good look at what *Princeton*'s planes had accomplished during the day.]

"At 1631 received the air operations plan for tomorrow as follows:

"Four VF Combat Air Patrol and four VT A/S [anti-submarine] patrol and four VF in condition 11 [ready] from sunrise to sunset; 0630 USS *Langley*, 0930 USS *Langley*, 1230 USS *Princeton*, 1530 USS *Princeton*. [This referred to strikes from the carriers for the next day.]

"At 1643 received fuelling plan for tomorrow from OTC as follows . . .

[There technical information, referring to fuelling dispositions and places. The interesting point illustrated here is that even in modern warfare fleet commanders spent a good deal of their time worrying about fuelling their vessels. Twenty years earlier they had worried about coaling; these new ships like *Princeton* drank oil instead, but they consumed it in vast quantities, especially when steaming at perhaps 18 or 20 knots as in combat operations—and in even greater quantities when they increased speed to 25 knots and above as they would in chase of an enemy.]

"At 1755 completed recovery of A/S [anti-submarine] patrol and Combat Air Patrols Nos. 5C and 5AA.

"At 1758 received the following dispatch from OTC, which was published to the ship's company by order of the commanding officer.

"Well done. I have the best carrier pilots in the entire Navy.

"At 1801 set fleet speed 18 knots, and at 1804 commenced zig-zagging . . . [as the ships did in night formation.]"

So the day was done at 1801, just after six o'clock in the evening. It had been a busy day, with one companion, Lt. (jg) Buckelew, lost in action, doing his duty for his country. But *Princeton* had been lucky that day for only one pilot had gone down. There would be other days when more would be lost, sad hard days ahead in this terrible war. For today, *Princeton* had done her duty. She had smashed the Japanese defenses on Wotje and the burning of the ammunition dumps had left the enemy short of supplies. That was the purpose of these attacks. Soften them up was the way it was usually put, and the softening process was to go on endlessly against the islands of the enemy.

Now, as night began to lower, the activity aboard *Princeton* did not cease, for a carrier never sleeps. There were parts to be replaced, machine shop work to be done, planes to be armed, and gasoline to be readied.

There was food to be prepared, and intelligence work to be done, and reports to be written by the pilots and the air intelligence officers. Someone had to take on the sad task of gathering together Lieutenant Buckelew's pitiful little handful of belongings; someone had to write a letter;

someone had to callously request replacement of a lost pilot. But that was war, that was the way it was. The ice-cream bar was open, the smoking lamp was lit. It was evening, the hardness of night had not yet set in with its ever-present dangers. It was the end of a good day for *Princeton*.

CHAPTER TWO

Stout Ship

Princeton was a stout ship and a happy one. She operated with the fast carriers and her planes and her men did their jobs well. Admiral Mitscher's commendations came along regularly, and Mitscher and his staff were not uncritical observers of their carriers. The Admiral was a tough taskmaster, and he would not hesitate to remove a Task Group Commander, or even order the replacement of a captain if he found something amiss. The rule of thumb was that a man got one chance, and if he did not make it, the rigors of war were such that he could not be used again. There was no place for failure in the Pacific in 1943 and 1944.

By February, 1944, *Princeton* and her crew were old hands at the business of fighting the Japanese. Early in February she was out with the Task Force, striking Japanese installations on Engibi Island and Eniwetok in the Marshalls—for that was to be the next big target of the fleet. After all, the landings had been made in the Marshalls, but it was a big chain, and the Japanese still controlled many islands. It would not do to have them build up their air strength and then be able to harry the ships in the lagoon at Roi Island Anchorage. One reason for securing the Marshalls was to get a big base where scores—even hundreds—of ships could be assembled and supplied for a jump-off to a farther point on the road to Japan. So *Princeton* had been out rat-killing, as they sometimes called it, preventing the Japanese from building up any strength for harassment. She had done her usual good job, and she and her men were happy and tired after four days of air strikes which ended on February 6.

That day Captain George Henderson had some news. It was good and bad: he was being promoted to command Fleet Air Wing One, a job that would demand all his aviation and administrative talents. But he was also being relieved as commander of the *Princeton*, and it is hard for a "plank owner"—one of those who put a ship in commission at the yard—to leave his command. It was even harder to leave *Princeton* for she was new and proud and every inch a fighting ship, steaming confidently into enemy waters day after day.

Relieving Captain Henderson was Captain William H. Buracker, who was waiting at Roi Anchorage. There was no sentimentality in the navy—there would be no series of festivities to honor the old captain and welcome the new one. Not at all: the orders came prosaically from Task Group: on arrival Roi Anchorage Captain Buracker would come aboard, and Captain Henderson would go ashore. Captain Henderson had all the warning he could expect—almost a full day. *Princeton* was at sea, steaming toward Roi when the orders came in at 1235. They would not anchor until 1055 the next morning.

Next day *Princeton* picked up her pilot at 1005 in the morning just outside the harbor, and the pilot brought with him secret charts that showed the mine fields and other protections. For this harbor was too important in the American plan to be left unguarded; even the American fighting ships had to be brought in by pilots so they would not go astray on the mine fields or protective devices.

At noon, Captain Henderson went over to the *Saratoga* for a last visit with the admiral, then returned at three o'clock in the afternoon; he said his last goodbyes to his shipmates. Five minutes later he stood on the quarterdeck and read his orders, detaching him from command. Then up stepped Captain Buracker and read his orders, which directed him to take command.

"Before the departure of Commodore Henderson," he said, "I wish to thank the *Princeton* for its outstanding performance of duty on this operation as well as on all operations since you have joined Carrier Division Eleven. To me you have no equal in the CVL [light carrier] class. Captain Henderson's superior leadership and your loyalty and efficiency have made it so. I know that you will always maintain those high standards of efficiency."

It was an apt statement, letting the crew know that the old captain had been promoted to Commodore, that Buracker was proud to come to *Princeton,* and that he intended to run a tight ship here.

Then the ceremony was over. Commodore Henderson squared his shoulders and was piped over the side of his ship. The boat swung away toward shore, he waved and some aboard waved back, and he was gone, and it was back to the war.

To succeed Captain Henderson, William Buracker was an admirable choice. He was a Virginia boy, soft-spoken, of medium height and build, neither handsome nor unhandsome, with a square jaw and the look of determination in eyes that otherwise might seem very mild.

He was William Houck Buracker, born in Luray, Virginia, on July 25, 1897, the son of William S. Buracker. He went to public schools in Virginia and in 1916 received an appointment to the United States Naval Academy. He went to Annapolis, but in 1917 found himself at sea, serving that summer on the battleship *Texas*. Back to school at Annapolis for the winter, and then to sea again the following spring, on the *New Hampshire* this time, one of the old battlewagons, one of the training grounds for young officers of the surface fleet.

After graduation from the Academy, Buracker was assigned to the USS *Mississippi,* another battleship, but in 1920 he went to destroyers, to the USS *Woolsey* and to the

Pacific, which meant calls at exotic places, and headquarters in San Diego in those days. For two years he served mostly on destroyers, the old four-pipers, burning their foul-smelling coal, and dirtying up the pristine whites of the most fastidious officers with their smoke. Then in 1922 he was returned to the Continental United States from sea duty, for he had requested and been granted flight training. He had been watching the growth of air power in the world, and was one of those who wanted to be a part of naval air.

At Pensacola, Ensign Buracker took the usual course of ground and air training, and soloed, and satisfied his instructors that he could fly. He was designated a Naval Aviator on December 21, 1922, and got his gold wings. After leave he was assigned to Scouting Squadron One, and later went to the Naval Air Station at Pearl Harbor, where he stayed until 1928. His work was good and well appreciated in the Navy—he was selected for the postgraduate course at the Naval Academy, and in 1928 went there to study aeronautical engineering. He was an apt student, and soon was sent to the Massachusetts Institute of Technology, where he was given the degree of Master of Science.

Always he was a leader. He served again with a patrol squadron in the big flying boats, but then went to Washington with the Plans Division of the Bureau of Aeronautics. While there he distinguished himself as one of the pilots of the six navy patrol planes to make a non-stop flight from Hampton Roads, Virginia, to the Canal Zone. That *was* an accomplishment in 1933, and it was all done in formation, too. For this job, Buracker received personal commendation from President Franklin D. Roosevelt.

In 1934 Buracker was a member of an observation squadron attached to the *West Virginia;* two years later he had his first command, Torpedo Squadron 2-B, based on the carrier *Saratoga*. This was his first carrier experience down from the big flying boats to the smaller planes. He led the squadron for a year, then was selected for the

Naval War College at Newport, Rhode Island, in the summer of 1937. There followed a tour of duty with the Army Air Corps at its tactical school at Maxwell Field, Alabama. Back in carriers, he served as navigator of the *Enterprise* and then took a staff job with the commander of aircraft of the battle force, and that is where he was when the Japanese bombed Pearl Harbor.

Captain Buracker had won the Silver Star, one of the nation's highest medals, for his conduct in the early raids on Marcus and the Marshall and Gilbert Islands, when the United States was fighting on a shoestring. He was given credit for saving the carrier from harm in the Marshalls engagement, "largely due to his skill and determination under fire."

But after this commendation, and a Unit Citation, Captain Buracker got a shore job—the bane of the existence of fighting sailors and airmen. He was beached—sent to the naval station at Pensacola as executive officer. Certainly it was important work, training the youngsters to fight was a part of it—but it wasn't fighting and that is what men like Buracker wanted in this war. That was their duty. But it was also their duty to obey orders, and like a good sailor, Buracker did his job.

He was a bright officer. His record showed it, for he was being groomed for high command. He went to the Army's staff school at Fort Leavenworth, and then to the Army Air Force School at Orlando, Florida, and the Army and Navy Staff College in Washington. Then, in October, 1943, he was sent to the Pacific, to join Admiral Nimitz's staff. There he stayed, until February, when he managed to get the command he had always wanted—the *Princeton*.

So it was off with the old and on with the new, and the war continued. By seven o'clock that night, the ship was moving along in its routine, sucking in 245,000 gallons of fuel oil and 38,000 gallons of aviation gasoline from the oiler *Millicoma*.

And there was a war—and out here in the Marshalls there was no forgetting it.

The fleet's radar screens picked up a bogie—unidentified—at 9:27 that night, and the ship went to general quarters along with every other vessel in the harbor. But if it was a snooper it was no more than that—a Japanese observation plane trying to find out what the American plans might be—and within an hour the "all clear" was sounded, and by 11 o'clock that night the ship was quiet again.

The next few days were taken up with resupply, for the *Princeton* had been a busy ship in the last few weeks and she needed many things. For one thing, she needed replacements, two torpedo planes and one fighter to bring the squadrons up to strength. These planes were supplied by fleet, through the "jeep" carriers, those little ships of all work of the carrier fleet, built on the hulls of tankers or merchant ships, used for ferrying and for anti-submarine warfare and for convoy protection.

There was housekeeping to be done. Planes damaged in recent actions were loaded aboard an LST that came alongside. They would be taken ashore and repaired or salvaged—it was a job for the leisure of the men at a base, not a job for carrier men. The job was done early on the morning of February 9: one torpedo bomber, one fighter, and two airplane engines were taken off, along with a miscellany of material that the sailors classified as junk. That day the *Princeton* sailed again, with the task group, and made her planes ready for action.

Late in the afternoon, *Princeton* launched her planes, Combat Air Patrol, over Engebi Island, and anti-submarine patrol. Just before dark, around 6:45 in the evening, the planes came home. One, a VF-14, a fighter, crashed into the number one barrier, damaging the plane slightly but not hurting the pilot. But that was the only excitement, and it was no tragedy.

This was *Princeton*'s birthday—the first anniversary of her commissioning, and the ship was celebrating. There were programs, and a special issue of the ship's paper, and a special dinner for all messes, with all the trimmings. The statistics, run up for the occasion, showed what a marvelous fighting machine *Princeton* really was and how staggering the full impact of the American war effort.

She had steamed 70,000 miles by this time, using nearly seven million gallons of fuel oil, and her planes had used 660,000 gallons of gasoline. She (her planes) had dropped 440,000 pounds of bombs, and shot off 18,000 rounds of 40mm ammunition and 38,000 rounds of 20mm ammunition from the anti-aircraft guns, in training and in battle. She had participated in 44 air strikes against the enemy, her planes had shot down (and she had shot some herself) 26 Japanese planes. She was responsible for the sinking of three enemy ships, too.

It was quite a record for a new carrier, and it showed how the war was going.

As the Americans moved closer to Japan that winter, the going got rougher, and by the end of March, when the Palaus were under attack, the Japanese were good and tough.

That afternoon, *Yorktown* reported shooting down a Japanese patrol bomber, a *Betty*, and the fleet then assumed that it had been discovered on the eve of the attack. That would mean increased opposition, of course, but there was nothing to be done about it. On the night of March 29, they kept a sharp lookout, and zig-zagged for safety as they did at night. Everyone was on edge.

Langley and *Princeton* were assigned to put up the Combat Air Patrol planes that evening, for protection of the fast moving fleet. The Task Force was nervous, no doubt about it, the speed of the force was increased to 23 knots, which made it a harder target for a submarine. But the question of air attack continued.

Local sunset was scheduled that day for just after eight o'clock. At eleven minutes after seven the order came to launch more planes, because a group of unidentified bogies had been spotted on the radar screen, ninety miles away, coming in from the northwest. The trouble was—at this time of day—that the planes of the Combat Air Patrol and anti-submarine patrol were running low on gas, and should be picked up before dark. These were not night fighters, there were very few night fighters in the fleet, and most pilots had little or no night experience. Therefore, any planes in the air after dark were in danger of crashing, or being forced to land in the water. The pilot's chances in any water landing were not so good as to make one comfortable.

Out in front of the fleet, the destroyer *Charles S. Ausburne* was acting as picket boat. It was a dangerous job—she had to stay alert all night, keep an eye out for blips on land and sea—and be prepared to warn the Task Force of anything unusual.

Twenty minutes after the first warning, the *Princeton*'s crew was called to General Quarters. They *were* Japanese out there, and they were coming in. Every man went to his action station, and a strange, almost quiet came over the big, rumbling ship, and she moved along swiftly through the water. Zig-zag-zig-zag—the *Princeton*'s quartermasters changed the course with a monotonous regularity heading generally a little north of west.

Then they saw them! One of the lookouts caught a glimpse and then another of five enemy planes flying very low on the red horizon of the setting sun, dipping beneath the horizon from time to time, waggling, and then coming back again. They crossed ahead of the formation, about twelve miles out.

From Task Force came the order: stop the zig-zagging, resume the base course almost west, and prepare for imminent air attack.

But Captain Buracker did not think the attack would come just yet. The smart thing for the Japanese to do—and they were very good at it—would be to wait, hold their planes in the air, and come in just after dark when the ships were least able to protect themselves.

Langley had the Combat Air Patrol that evening, and she kept those planes in the air just as long as she could—but eventually they had to come down, eventually and before dark. She began recovering just before eight o'clock, and then spread the news that her planes had shot down one Japanese medium bomber outside the defense perimeter. Actually, the men of *Princeton* did not need that word—they could see the smoke of the plane as it plunged into the sea, even in the growing darkness. Another was reported, shot down by planes from *Wasp*, but she was too far away for *Princeton*'s crew to make out the action.

At eight minutes after eight *Princeton*'s watchers reported an unidentified aircraft off to the west, out 12 miles. At nineteen after eight, the last of *Langley*'s "chickens" came home to roost—eighteen minutes after sunset. They were playing it very close that night. Now they had no "eyes" above, and if there was an attack the basic defense would be maneuvering and anti-aircraft guns. Here was the carrier at its most vulnerable.

Admiral Mitscher kept changing the speed of the fleet—23 knots—21 knots—18 knots—23 knots. The purpose was to confuse the enemy, and relieve the danger of submarine attack.

But the planes were coming in now.

At 8:45, unidentified planes were reported moving in from the southeast, out 22 miles.

Fleet speed was changed to 23 knots.

Nine minutes later the fleet turned left, putting the Japanese planes astern, and just then the various ships opened up their guns as the planes began to move into range.

They were coming in very low, some of them heading straight, some of them waggling and taking evasive action against the flak.

Pom-pom-pom-pom went the fast-firing guns.

Bomp—bomp—went the heavier anti-aircraft.

Puffs of black and white snuggled around the incoming Japanese planes, still visible in the fading light.

There was a flash of fire, a burst of smoke—and then a steady licking of flames at one of the planes. It turned, right wing down, over onto its back, and gracefully peeled off into the sea—a Japanese hero going to his death.

On they came, heading for *Princeton* and the other ships. They were torpedo bombers, that much was sure. The lookouts strained their eyes for that fatal wake, but saw nothing.

One plane seemed to choose the *Princeton* as its target and came boring in. With detailed concentration, the men at the anti-aircraft guns sighted in on the Japanese plane, that two-engined bomber, coming in so gracefully on the port quarter.

Pom-pom-pom.

Boomp—boomp.

There! Someone had gotten a hit. One engine flamed up, and lit the sky for the gunners.

But in came the Japanese with the singlemindedness of the trained combat pilot. He wanted to launch that fish—and if he could not launch he might just ram it into the side of *Princeton*.

In he came, and there was no question now about his destination. It *was* the *Princeton*.

At two thousand yards, more than a mile, one could almost see the determination of the pilot as he nursed his flaming engine and headed in low and straight, angling for the port quarter of the light carrier.

Fifteen hundreds yards. The ack-ack was bursting around him—they must be getting hits—but on he came, boring in.

A thousand yards. The smoke of the shells threaded across his wings, and when a big one hit close, the plane seemed to jump—but still he came boring in, boring in, boring in. It was enough—this determination—to give a youngster a queesy feeling in the stomach.

Seven hundred and fifty yards. He looked big now, much bigger than usual. Then . . .

Five hundred yards. In a few seconds he would be on them.

Pom-pom-pompompompompom chattered the 20 millimeters.

Poom-poom-poom went the 40s.

Then a white flash lit up the darkening sky, and the plane disintegrated in mid-air.

They had hit the gas tank or the torpedo.

Suddenly it was quiet for a few seconds. Very quiet on the deck.

But then, another plane came in and the guns began once more to chatter their talk of death.

The lookouts strained now in the darkness for signs of torpedos. Planes were whizzing by the ships, and one came across from port to stern, close by the bow.

Had he dropped.

The forward lookouts peered.

Nothing.

Then he was gone, even the sound of him was gone. The guns stopped firing, and the quiet of night at sea descended once more on the *Princeton*.

In a little while it was apparent that the attack was over and there was little probability there would be another. The danger this night would be from submarines, and were the roles of the adversaries reversed, it would have been a serious danger. But the Japanese had long misused their submarine fleet—converting it from an attack weapon to a resupply force, with relatively few submarines on the prowl. The lookouts were there, but since few of the Japanese submarines were in the area, there did not seem much chance of trouble from that quarter.

The ship settled down to its night-time routine, changing the watches. There were reports to be made, old and new—for this evening's action called for a new report: every time a gun was fired aboard the *Princeton* there had to be a report. One hundred thirty-nine rounds of 40mm ammunition and 353 rounds of 20 millimeter. That's what it had taken to down that Japanese plane, and scare off the other one.

The fleet swished through the night, changing course now and again, changing speed, and the destroyer screen, which had moved in tight next to the ships during the action, moved out to six thousand yards, more than three miles, to take a wider sweep. The fleet settled down, *Princeton*'s officer of the deck ordered the lower deck spaces ventilated.

At 11:40 the destroyer *Frazier* reported sighting a single plane close aboard, and the Task Force went to General Quarters again.

But absolutely nothing happened. The plane was not confirmed by any other ship. Either it was a bit of someone's active imagination aboard *Frazier,* or it was one of the night snoopers, the big flying boats the Japanese seemed to keep in the air all the time to dog the Americans. No one ever knew which.

The strike against the Palau Islands was scheduled for dawn, but at five o'clock in the morning, an hour and a half before dawn, *Lexington* and *Yorktown* launched night fighters—a protective measure so they might sweep the air around them and make sure that no Japanese force was waiting to swoop down on the carriers when their decks were loaded with planes not yet in the air.

Princeton headed into the wind at 6:33, and began launching in the predawn darkness two minutes later. In fifteen minutes she put up a dozen fighters to make the first fighter sweep across the Palau Islands.

Again it was her responsibility to protect the fleet. At 7:14 she was launching eight fighters that would go up for Combat Air Patrol, circulating the force, and six torpedo bombers, loaded with anti-submarine weapons, watching for submarines.

Sunrise came at eight o'clock, and operations were well under way. The planes from *Princeton* returned from that first strike at 9:48, sighting a pilot in a rubber raft on their way home. They put out the word, and the search began for the pilot, whoever he was. It was one of the characteristics of the carrier team that when a rubber raft was seen, a destroyer or an escort vessel went out to hunt—because of all the weapons the United States Navy considered, its most valuable were the men themselves.

The celerity with which the navy acted was shown that day. The second strike against the Palau Islands was launched by *Princeton* in the morning, and a third strike at noon. At three o'clock in the afternoon, one of *Princeton*'s planes straggling home after having been hit by a fire, plunged into the water 2,000 yards from the ship. The pilot could not make it all the way back.

Immediately the destroyer *Stanly* moved around from behind, to pick up the pilot, who was lucky enough to get out of his plane and into his raft. That was how it went. If the pilot could bring his plane back near the force, and if he could survive his landing, his chances of coming home again were really quite good. Iffy—but everything in this Pacific war was iffy, for that matter.

In this case, the pilot was Lt. (jg) J.M. Webb—a very lucky young man. From the time that he crashlanded until he was aboard the destroyer was exactly twenty-four minutes.

There was plenty of excitement. All day long *Princeton* launched and recovered planes. One plane developed trouble and crash-landed just after taking off, back on the carrier. It was moved away from the landing zone. At four o'clock in the afternoon, a torpedo bomber was launched on a mission, and then had to turn back and land, because the radio operator had been injured—striking the transformer in the rush of catapulting. He had to be taken out of the plane and sent to sick bay and replaced. Then the bomber was recatapulted to proceed on its mission.

Again as evening closed in, the men of *Princeton* grew nervous, because this was the time that the Japanese became most active. Sure enough, at 7:50 that night, unidentified aircraft were sighted again, and the story of the night before seemed ready to be repeated.

Five minutes later the men of *Princeton* saw their Japanese snooper, a big bomber flying at 20,000 feet. From there, in the failing light of day, he could get a good view of the whole Task Force. He was at 20,000 feet because there he was almost safe—even the big guns of the battleships were not likely to bring him down at that distance. He crossed gracefully over to port, and disappeared in the cloud cover. But on *Princeton*, Captain Buracker and the men knew that it might only be the beginning of the evening action.

But tonight it was quiet, and it was several hours before Captain Buracker learned why.

The Japanese had been coming in all right, planning their attack for just after sunset. There had been nine of them; nine graceful Bettys with the torpedoes slung under their nacelles. And that they had run afoul of the Combat Air Patrol planes of *Cabot*, which were low on fuel and nearly ready to return.

Not one Betty went home that night. *Cabot*'s score was nine out of nine, and the bombers lived up to the name the Japanese pilots had ironically given them at home, "flaming lighters," because they caught fire so very easily. Once, just a few short months ago, a formation of nine Bettys would have been accompanied by a swarm of Zero fighters and would have been a formidable opponent; but it was a measure of the way the war was going, this 9 of 9 tonight. The constant pounding of the Japanese air pipeline by *Princeton* and the other carriers was taking its toll. The Japanese were losing planes by the thousands (they lost four thousand planes in the Guadalcanal campaign, for example). Japanese plane building was still going on, but the effect of the carrier strikes was being felt more every day.

The Japanese came out again that night, with the ferocity of desperation, but they did not come near *Princeton*, nor did they damage any other American ships. For *Princeton* it was, thankfully, a quiet night.

Next day, there was a little of a new kind of excitement. The destroyer *Mertz* sighted a small Japanese merchant ship, a sixty-foot vessel that was more properly a boat than a ship at all, a wooden boat at that. It was the kind of vessel that the Japanese used frequently in their inter-island traffic, sometimes carrying quantities of valuable materials. As the war progressed, Japan reverted more and more to these ships in an effort to escape the attention of the American submarines and planes. This poor captain this day was definitely in the wrong place at the wrong time. After a few minutes of gunfire from the destroyer, the boat was left sinking, and two survivors were taken aboard the *Mertz* to be delivered to Naval Intelligence.

Princeton's task this day was to supply planes for the attack on the Palau Islands and to keep up the Combat Air Patrol over a sector of the fleet. At 7:52 when the Combat Air Patrol was up, two Japanese planes were reported, forty to fifty miles out, and *Princeton*'s planes were assigned to bring them down. But the job went to the strike force, because they were on the way, and by making a little detour they could smash the Japanese and then go about their business. A few minutes later they had done the job: "one Betty splashed"—the other got away. And it was still a minute before sunrise.

Less than an hour later the CAP (Combat Air Patrol) had its chance. The radar men reported another blip coming in—this time close by the ship—and the fighters were directed out to the vicinity of the enemy. "Splash another Betty" was the message that came back a few minutes later.

Princeton had a fright that day—a fright and a little tragedy. Around 11 o'clock the planes began to come in from the strike and from the Combat Air Patrol. By 11:15 all planes had landed—and *Princeton* was short six "chickens." Had she lost six pilots and six planes? Everyone aboard began to wonder.

A message to the fleet gave comfort, because the reply came back from *Bunker Hill* that five of the boys were there, having landed on this carrier because she was close, and they had expended nearly all their gasoline. But as for the sixth man—the story was more tragic. He had been seen to be shot down over the target, and the only hope for his life—not his immediate recovery—was that he had been able to parachute safely into the lagoon, and would become a prisoner of the Japanese.

There was one chance that the pilot might be saved, and Admiral Sam Ginder, Commander of the task group, decided to take it. He ordered up two seaplanes from the USS *Alabama* to try to rescue the pilot, if he could be found in the lagoon. That meant going in under the eyes and guns of the Japanese. The planes were launched at 1:53 that afternoon, with *Princeton* putting up four fighters which would circle the area and cover the rescue attempt. The search continued for nearly seven hours before it was abandoned—unsuccessful.

Meanwhile, *Princeton* went about her military business, launching and recovering planes. One of the pilots who had landed on the *Bunker Hill* was wounded, so he remained on that ship. The others came back during the course of the day.

In the middle of the afternoon, *Princeton* developed some mechanical troubles in her main condenser and secured the number two shaft for two hours to repair. This meant the whole task group had to slow down to 16 knots to keep *Princeton* in formation. It was done, with extra special care being taken to look out for submarines at this lower speed.

The target for the next day, the men of *Princeton* learned, would be Woleai, and so the maps and charts were brought out and studied by the navigator and the intelligence officers that afternoon, while the operations continued. The day sped by, and air operations came to an end, except the rescue mission, just before six o'clock. One of the fighters flying cover for the seaplanes came in and crashed into a barrier wire, damaging the plane but not hurting the ship or any personnel.

That was the last excitement of the day—or nearly so. The ship settled down for the night, and the zig-zagging began, and then came a report that *Yorktown* had passed a floating object that might be a mine. *Princeton* sheered off to the right to avoid it, did so, and steamed on, into the quiet tropical night that would have seemed so peaceful under any other conditions.

CHAPTER THREE

The Big Battle

The carriers were in and out of battle all spring. On May 12, *Princeton* was moored in Berth V-2 at Pearl Harbor, when an important change took place, an historic change in a sense. On that day, Lieutenant M.T. Hatcher had the happy and sad duty of telling his pilots and crewmen that Air Group 23 was being moved off the ship. It was sad news, because it meant the end of a period in the lives of all these men. It was delightful news because the orders of Air Group 23 were to transfer to the USS *Altamaha*, a transport, for transportation to the West Coast. There they would report to "Commander, Fleet Air Wings, West Coast, for leave rehabilitation, and reforming." That last brought cheers from the 38 officers, and 51 enlisted men of the Air Group. Home leave? It was hard to believe, after nearly a year and a half of gruelling duty. They had flown thousands of training and war missions since February 25, 1943, and they were plank owners of the *Princeton*, but they were going home.

Replacing them was Air Group 27, consisting of Fighting Squadron Twenty Seven and Torpedo Squadron Twenty Seven, the two Squadrons under command of Lt. Comdr. E.W. Wood Jr., a regular navy pilot.

On May 15, *Princeton* set out with *Yorktown* and *Monterey* for training exercises to break in the new air

31

crews. Rear Admiral Ralph Davison, one of Nimitz' "fighting admirals" was in charge of the Task Group and he was going to make sure the men were ready to go into battle. One of the major differences these days between American fliers in the Pacific and their enemy was the degree and competence of their training. The Americans were trained "to a gnat's eyelash" and now they were going out for air operations and gunnery practice, in the Hawaiian area. By this time—the spring of 1944—the Japanese were hard put to conduct any training at all. One problem was shortage of instructors—many competent Japanese pilots had been shot down in the past few months. The Japanese did not rotate their air crews: a man went to the front and stayed there to outlast the war or die. Another problem for the Japanese was drastic shortage of aviation fuel and oil for their ships. They could not sortie outside the Inland Sea because they did not have the fuel.

They practiced takeoffs and landings until Captain Buracker and Lt. Comdr. Wood were satisfied that the *Princeton*'s fliers were up to snuff.

Then it was back to Pearl for minor repairs, and on May 29, departure for Majuro Atoll to rejoin the fast Carrier Task Force and begin operations against the Japanese again. The invasion of the Marianas was about to begin, and the carriers were needed to undertake their now famous "softening-up" process.

Princeton joined up with task group 58.3 on June 6, to start the air raids against Saipan and the other islands. On June 11, she launched a sweep of fighters against Saipan. The tension began to rise.

Early on the morning of June 12, the Japanese snoopers began to arrive over the fleet, dropping flares, and harrying the task groups. At 3:30 in the morning one plane dropped nine flares on the port bow of the *Princeton,* and, of course, Captain Buracker doubled the alert against possible torpedo or air attack, even in this middle of the night-time hours. For the rest of the night, the *Princeton* was busy, shooting and maneuvering, watchful for any tricks the enemy might try to play.

Enterprise and other carriers launched fighters at 4:15 in the morning, long before sunrise, but *Princeton* began operations after the sun came up at 5:41 that day. The Combat Air Patrol distinguished itself around nine o'clock in the morning, when a "bogie" was sighted first by the battleship *Alabama*. It turned out to be a twin-engine Japanese fighter, a "Nick." *Princeton*'s air patrol teamed up on the Nick, and shot it down in about three minutes. Operations were routine that day, thereafter, except for one sound contact which indicated a submarine was in the area—or it might have been a whale. In any event, there was no trouble undersea.

On the next day the *Princeton*'s planes were busy striking Saipan along with three of the rest of the test group, and at 1025 that morning, the ship's crew caught sight of the island as the *Princeton* came in close.

They watched the battleships bombard the island, and pass through oil drums and other debris that must have represented sunken ships. Some one hundred Japanese sailors were picked out of the water by destroyers about that time, and some were taken to the *Lexington* for interrogation. Among those survivors that day were three laborers who carried American identification from Guam Naval Base.

Princeton, the other carriers, and the battleships left Saipan smoking, and the flotsam from a dozen sunken fishing boats behind them that day, and moved on to strike Guam on June 14. The next day it was back to Saipan to make strikes in support of the landings there. The Japanese threw in some air power this day, and a Japanese fighter was shot down by *Princeton*'s Combat Air Patrol about six o'clock that evening, forty-three miles out from the carrier. That plane was a command plane, Captain Buracker soon learned from task group—the air intelligence officer reported that the pilot had ordered an attack on the task group just before he was shot down, and sure enough it was not long before a group of bogies appeared on the radar screens. The Japanese were up to their old tricks, coming in by evening.

Then the action began in earnest. At 6:19, *Princeton* reported planes coming in from the southwest, fifty-two miles out. Soon another group was spotted, coming from the southeast. Planes of all the carriers were in the air, and the fighting began within a few minutes. At 6:39 *San Jacinto*'s planes shot down three Japanese, apparently fighters carrying small bombs—an indication of the condition of the Japanese air force in the area.

In all, *Princeton* counted four raids, coming in from different directions, and then at 7 o'clock at night came a fifth raid. Not one came near the *Princeton*, until seven minutes past seven when the lookouts sighted seven Japanese planes just above the horizon, dead ahead of the task group. The ships opened fire with their anti-aircraft guns, and the formation turned left to the east. The Japanese planes moved in swiftly, but the anti-aircraft fire was too much for them. Down they went, one, two, three, four, five, six—flamers all of them. The seventh plane did not burn, but swooped down, cartwheeled and skidded into the water, then sank. They had done nothing of note—except to cause some damage when anti-aircraft fire from some ships hit other ships.

Princeton had suffered thus. She took at least five 40mm shells from screening battleships during the melee, and one of the shells penetrated the skin of the ship below the water line and flooded the two forward peak tanks and the forward fresh water pump room. Five officers and six enlisted men were injured, two of them critically.

Damage control and the medics were on the job taking the men below, and treating their wounds, and cleaning up the damage below decks. Above, the men of *Princeton* were still fighting because Raid VI closed in. And now, came more raids, lasting until after dark, as usual.

On June 16, the damage control teams were still working to repair the ravages of the night before. Compartment

A-402-A was pumped dry and the shell hole was plugged up. Operations continued that day, with one big, and exciting change. It was rumored that the Japanese fleet was out, from which the Japanese were expected to come, but they found nothing that day.

The battle developed on June 19, although not quite as had been expected. The Japanese seemed to be willing to risk a fleet engagement, but they were not quite doing so this day.

The affair began at two o'clock in the morning, when *Enterprise* and *Lexington* launched search planes which would move out 275 miles to the west. But they found nothing that morning; the only excitement on *Princeton* was the loss of a man overboard, MM1c Edward Chong Wong. A float light and life ring were immediately thrown overboard after him, and destroyer pickets searched the area. But he was never found.

At 8:20 Admiral Mitscher ordered the attack on Guam to begin. *Princeton*'s role at the moment seemed minor: she was to keep up the Combat Air Patrol over the task group and also the anti-submarine patrol. But at ten minutes after ten that morning, the role changed, and *Princeton*'s pilots were thrown into the thick of the battle. The Japanese had launched an air strike from their unfound carriers, and were coming in, almost directly from the west. They were 150 miles out when discovered.

This would be the major Japanese effort, Captain Buracker was sure. Intelligence from submarine reports indicated that the Japanese had put a large force to sea, including carriers, which had come from the Philippines area a few days earlier.

Admiral Mitscher had been waiting. He moved fast now. He ordered all carriers to launch all available fighters.

On the *Princeton* the rush began. First the decks had to be cleared of the torpedo planes which were arming for strikes. The carrier had to be brought into the wind to launch, and she was, along with the rest of the fleet at 10:22.

The Japanese came in. At 10:23 some 30 planes were reported 110 miles out, closing in from the west.

10:30———72 miles out, and closing.

10:33———63 miles out, still closing.

10:36———still coming.

Admiral Mitscher sent a message to his Task Force then, and it was received on *Princeton*.

"Expect repeated attacks," it said. "Keep fighters available to repel these attacks landing planes as necessary."

10:38———*Princeton* now had 20 fighters and four torpedo bombers in the air.

10:39———the enemy was 48 miles out, still coming.

Just then the Japanese planes—an estimated 40 in number—were intercepted by *Princeton*'s Combat Air Patrol.

10:48———The Japanese were coming in. Other ships began to open fire.

10:49———Mitscher increased fleet speed to 22 knots.

10:50———The fleet turned to starboard.

10:55———The Japanese were now 15 miles out, still coming.

Now came reports of other groups of Japanese planes, coming in from various angles, south and west.

The fighting began for *Princeton* at 11:56 when a Japanese torpedo plane formation moved in against the task group. There was an explosion a moment later in the wake of the *Enterprise,* and *Princeton* turned hard right to move into the attacking planes, which were coming singly along the starboard beam, gliding in low, trying to get a shot with their torpedoes.

At 12:00 two Japanese torpedo planes attacked from the starboard, but the gunners of *Princeton* sent them both spinning into the sea. Two minutes later another Jap plane came in, and Captain Buracker turned hard right to face the enemy. The anti-aircraft gunners fired as fast as they could—the plane burst into flames, one wing fell off, and the rest fell into the water 600 yards off the starboard bow. The captain ordered hard left—to avoid the falling plane.

There was a heavy jarring noise—an underwater explosion—probably of the torpedo of this plane—but that was the only thing. There was no damage, to *Princeton* or to any other ship in the area.

Raids continued to come in, but *Princeton* was clear. She began recovering aircraft, including one from the *Bataan* which landed on *Princeton* low on gasoline.

American planes and American ships wreaked havoc with the Japanese that day. Raider after raider came in, and was shot down by the fighters or by anti-aircraft fire. Fifty-five miles out one whole Japanese formation of 20 planes was knocked down by fighters. And *Princeton*'s planes were in the fight, as the returning pilots began to report.

One torpedo plane on anti-submarine patrol had found a Japanese submarine just fifteen miles east of the task group. He had attacked with his depth charges, but unsuccessfully. He came back to his ship, but was driven off by anti-aircraft fire from nervous gunners in the fleet around him, and only much later, when affairs had quieted down did he land on *Princeton*.

Three divisions of F6F's of Group 27 were on Combat Air Patrol over the Task Force—that was their responsibility—when they were suddenly vectored out to intercept the formation of Japanese that was coming in. Here is their report:

"The enemy force consisted of 30 to 45 fighters, dive bombers, and torpedo bombers, flying at approximately 20,000 to 25,000 feet, about 40 miles from Task Force 58 when encountered. An air battle developed during which VF-27 planes shot down 15 enemy planes and accounted for three assists and one probable.

"At 10:25 two additional divisions of F6F's and VF-27 were launched and rectored toward a second wave of enemy aircraft. Of the estimated 30 to 40 enemy fighters, dive bombers, and torpedo planes, VF-27 pilots accounted for 14 more shot down, two assists, and five probables.

"On VF-27 pilot, Lieutenant Lamb, discovered a formation of 12 enemy torpedo planes previously unreported.

In spite of the fact that he was alone and had only one gun functioning, he flew formation on the enemy group, reported their location, course, and speed to the Task Force and then shot down three of the enemy aircraft before other friendly fighters arrived. He had previously shot down another enemy plane and scored a probable during the same air battle . . . One other VF-27 pilot, Lieutenant Brown, led his division to Rota airfield on instruction from his base and shot down an enemy plane preparing to land there later in the afternoon.''

By early afternoon the planes were coming home. The Combat Air Patrol reported shooting down one Japanese dive bomber at 2:47. But not all the news was so comforting. When the planes from the strike came in they brought some mournful information; the ship had lost her competent and respected air group commander, Lt. Comdr. Wood, and his wing man Lt. (jg) V.B. Carter. They were last seen by other *Princeton* pilots engaging a dozen Japanese dive bombers.

As for damage, the Task Force had suffered little. The battleship *South Dakota* took one bomb in the superstructure, but that did not impair the ship's fighting efficiency. Among the ships around *Princeton* that was all.

There was a quiet period now, and Captain Buracker used it to launch a search for Wood and Carter. Perhaps, he hoped, they had ditched and survived in their rafts. He sent out a fighter and a torpedo bomber to comb the area where they were last seen. But there was nothing.

The fighting continued all day, and in the evening, when Admiral Mitscher asked for a count of planes destroyed, the total came to more than 350 by all carriers. *Princeton* had certainly done her part. Her pilots had downed 27 Japanese planes and her anti-aircraft fire had shot down another three.

It was a good day for the carrier. Admiral Mitscher said so.

''The aviators and ships guns of this Task Force have

done a job today which will make their country proud of them," he said. "Their skillful defense of this Task Force enabled the force to escape a vicious well-coordinated air group attack carried out with determination."

It was high praise, but *Princeton* and the other ships deserved it. They had put another hole in the enemy's air power, in a battle that would go down in history as the "Marianas Turkey Shoots" because so many Japanese planes were destroyed.

Admiral Raymond Spruance, the commander of Fifth Fleet was urged by some to take after the Japanese this night, but he decided that his primary responsibility was to protect the American landings in the Marianas, and he did not wish to be drawn away from the area. Therefore, instead of turning west and chasing the Japanese carriers that night, Spruance led the fleet southeast, and then later changed the course to west, when it was decided that the Task Force would go after the Japanese surface forces.

That night, *Princeton* steamed along with the force at 23 knots, heading 260 degrees, trying to find the enemy. At four o'clock in the morning, Admiral Mitscher ordered the carriers to hold their flight groups on deck until the search planes had found the Japanese. But that too changed, and at 5:23 in the morning *Princeton*'s planes were in the air. Some Japanese planes were shot down that morning, but it did not mean very much in terms of the fleet disposition— because the Japanese had followed the technique of flying from the carriers, landing on the islands nearby, and shuttling back and forth. So one could hardly tell where the Japanese planes had come from.

In the afternoon a periscope was seen—but the Japanese fleet was not. But at 3:45 *Princeton* had the word that units of the Japanese navy had been sighted at 15 degrees 02' N, 135 degrees 25' E on a course of 270 degrees at a speed of 20 knots. That meant the Japanese were running away from them. Five minutes later, Captain Buracker had the order that all carriers were to stand by to launch strikes with the almost pure knowledge that they could not get back before dark. Two minutes later he had the information that the Japanese were disposed in three groups, consisting of battleships, carriers, cruisers, destroyers, and oilers—in other words the whole shebang. The carriers were the priority target, said Mitscher. Get those carriers.

Princeton was to join the second strike group with her planes, but after the first strike was launched, Mitscher decided it was too late in the day and cancelled the second strike. So *Princeton*'s pilots were excluded from the group that did find and strike the Japanese fleet that day.

She did participate in the recovery of planes. It was a hard job, because the planes came back late that night, after dark. *Princeton* and the others turned on their lights at 8:10, almost an hour after sunset, for the pilots were almost out of gas, and had been instructed to land on any carrier they saw. Three planes landed on *Princeton*, one from *Lexington*, one from *Yorktown*, and one from *Enterprise*. Many planes landed around the carrier, unable to make it with those last few drops of gas. By 10:54 it was finished—there were no more planes. The formation steamed through the same waters, the destroyers and escorts searching for survivors in their yellow rafts, and the rescues continued most of the night.

Next morning, *Princeton*'s captain secured permission to use those three fighters and other planes for the next strike on the Japanese. But the Japanese had been badly hurt in the strike of the day before. Three of their carriers were sunk, and they had no more taste for battle—nor did they have the planes with which to fight, following the beating they had taken on June 19. So there was no battle on June 21; the fleet moved back toward the Marianas, and the Japanese limped home. *Princeton* had done her job well once again.

There was more action during the next few days, especially on June 23.

One heroic incident involved Ensign W.G. Burgess, pilot of a torpedo plane on anti-submarine patrol. Here is the story from the squadron's action report:

"The torpedo plane was on its cross leg on a course of 238 degrees on a routine anti-submarine patrol . . . when the Betty was sighted by the radio man about four miles away at four o'clock, about fifty feet above the water. At the time of sighting, the Betty was . . . heading away from the formation. Its speed was estimated at 200 to 220 knots. The TRM-1C was at 800 feet, at a speed of 130 knots.

"Upon sighting the Betty the radio man proceeded to direct the pilot to the target and it was first sighted by the latter on his port side about one mile ahead and below. Ensign Burgess immediately nosed over and added throttle. At about the same time the Betty sighted the torpedo plane and added speed enough to open the distance to about two-and-a-half miles. With "everything to the fire wall" the TBM 1C, at a speed of 245 or 250 knots, started to gain on the Betty. Both planes were then at fifty feet in straight and level flight. It required several minutes to close the distance.

"When the torpedo plane overtook the Betty, the latter was on the starboard side, about ten feet off the water. Ensign Burgess made a low run on the port side of the enemy plane, firing with his twin .50 calibre wing guns. The Betty's port engine started smoking, but the guns jammed on the run, and Burgess pulled off to the Betty's port side at fifty feet and about one hundred feet from the Betty. During this run and retirement the turret gunner was apparently able to knock the enemy's turret gun.

Ensign Burgess was successful in getting his port gun back in commission, and he started a second run on the enemy. In this run he reported that his tracers seemed to by going into the Betty's port wing. All of his fire was tracer controlled since he had not installed his gun sight. Both the turret gun and the port wing gun jammed during this run, and Burgess decided it was time to change his tactics and splash the Betty without the aid of gunfire. He put his plane about two feet above the Betty and sat there in an attempt to force the Betty into the water. He succeeded in forcing the Betty to hit the water with her belly, but she immediately bounced back up to ten feet, her initial altitude, with no damaging results. Abandoning this procedure, Burgess retired to the Betty's starboard, and during retirement the TBM 1C's stinger was able to fire about thirty rounds into the after port side of the Betty's fuselage.

"Burgess next decided to adopt the Russian technique of chewing up the enemy plane with his propeller. This was also unsuccessful, although his prop came within inches of the Betty's starboard wing. Feeling somewhat frustrated, Burgess flew wing on the Betty with about two feet between wing tips. Burgess looked over at the Betty's pilot and waved, but the latter only toothed back at him. It was at this juncture that the turret gunner of the torpedo plane, in desperation, opened his hatch and emptied all six rounds of his .38 calibre revolver into the Betty with unobserved results on the enemy, but with great elation to the gunner.

"Tiring of this, Ensign Burgess crossed over top of the enemy plane and retired to about a quarter of a mile away on the Betty's port side. He managed to get his starboard wing gun charged, and he made a pass at the Betty's port side. This time his tracers went into the starboard engine, and it burst into flames. The flames spread to the starboard wing, the Betty lost control, her port wing dipped into the water, and the enemy plane executed a neat cartwheel. Ensign Burgess saw one survivor in the water after the Betty was splashed and this one was picked up almost immediately by a friendly [to the U.S.] destroyer.

"The battle between the Betty and the torpedo plane lasted about seven minutes. The damage to the torpedo plane consisted of seven 7.7mm holes, one through the radioman's compartment and the remainder through the port wing."

CHAPTER FOUR

The Sho Plan

The Japanese fleet was lying doggo—and the Americans coursed the Pacific that summer of 1944, laying waste to Japanese islands and airfields, striking Japanese shipping at will, and creating havoc where they went. On July 9, *Princeton* was with the fast Carrier Task Force at anchor in Eniwetok for resupply and replacement of planes. Five days later she was sailing again, to the Marianas to furnish air support for the occupation of Guam and Tinian islands. For four days the pilots of *Princeton* struck at Guam, bombing the air fields and looking for targets.

The main idea was to keep the Japanese from using their air fields on Guam and Rota, and the way to keep them down was to make so many large craters in the runways that they could not fly from them. The Japanese on the ground were dedicated and efficient men, but they could not keep up with the constant plastering of the runways by the American bombers. But *Princeton* did not get off totally unscathed. One pilot was hit by anti-aircraft fire and lost.

By August 2, this action was finished and *Princeton* was back at Eniwetok for upkeep, some work on her boilers, and resupply once again. She took on some new crew, and then went out for some training in the waters around the Marshalls before heading for the Philippines. It was the end of August.

The new air commander, following the loss of Lt. Comdr. Wood, was Lt. Comdr. F.A. Bardshar, described by Captain Buracker as a fine leader. The training topped off the work of a well-trained air group, and now, under Admiral William F. Halsey, *Princeton* was prepared to go back into action as part of Task Force 38. Vice Admiral Marc Mitscher was still commanding the Task Force, part of Third Fleet, and Rear Admiral Frederick C. Sherman was commander of Task Group 38.3, to which *Princeton* now belonged.

The first move was to the Palau area, where the job was again "softening-up." On September 7 and 8 *Princeton*'s planes hit the Japanese there, and then moved west and on the ninth and tenth of the month made the first carrier air strikes on Mindanao in the Philippines. It was not long then, before the Japanese realized what was coming, and made ready to activate their SHO (Victory) Operation, which was to call for the movement of the Japanese fleet into the waters where the Americans invaded next. The next strikes in which *Princeton* participated were against the Visayas, the Central Philippines. These strikes were in support of the Palau landings too, and they gave further indication to the Japanese that something big would be coming.

Admiral Halsey led the Third Fleet again to the Philippines on September 21 and 22, to conduct the first carrier strikes on Luzon, the main Philippine center, and principally on Manila. *Princeton* was given the very important job of making the first fighter sweep against the Japanese fields in the Manila area. They considered their task the hottest one of the day, and they were very pleased to have been chosen. They did a fine job and were commanded by Captain Buracker and Admiral Mitscher. Indeed they deserved it: they had knocked down 38 enemy planes with a loss of only one of their own. And that loss was not permanent: Lieutenant W.E. Lamb, the executive officer of the fighter squadron of *Princeton*'s Air Group 23, was hit and had to make a forced landing in Taal lake, about sixty miles south of Manila. But fighters from *Princeton* and other carriers circled him as he went in. They saw him being rescued by some men in a small boat. It appeared that they were not Japanese but Filipinos, and that fact was a great comfort to the men of *Princeton*, although they could not be precisely certain of events.

In fact, Lieutenant Lamb was rescued. He went into the lake, was pulled out by natives, taken to the guerrillas and kept there, treated like a lord for seven weeks, until he could be brought out. When he finally did come out, he brought with him some very valuable intelligence information for the army and navy.

So the result of the first big sweep at Manila was perfect as far as *Princeton* went: 38 kills and no losses.

It had been quite a day, starting with a strafing run at Nichols field, the major Japanese base near Manila, and then continuing to sweep over Manila harbor and Cavite naval base. Finally they hit Laguna de Bay, southeast of Manila, and even if five planes were damaged in the affray, considering what might have been—what would have been only a few months before when Japanese air forces were at their fighting peak—*Princeton* had a right to crow.

It was a busy time. *Princeton* and the other carriers moved offshore to refuel, and then came boring back in on the Philippines. They bombed Coron, Masbate, and made a fighter sweep over Panay and Negros Islands where the Japanese maintained important air fields. The Coron strike was notable because it was launched at a greater distance from the target than any previous strike from *Princeton*. The round trip for the pilots was more than 700 miles— which was a long, long way. But the distance was helpful in creating surprise. *Princeton*'s planes found three large ships at Coron Island, a favorite Japanese transit base, and left one oiler sinking, black smoke and flames shooting up from the bow, and the stern under water. There was not much doubt about that one. The planes also damaged a medium-sized cargo ship, but did not manage to sink her.

At Masbato they attacked more cargo ships. They left one big cargo ship dead in the water, and three smaller ones badly damaged. Here, one *Princeton* aviator made a forced water landing about five miles west of Milagros, and was later rescued by a Kingfisher observation plane from the battleship *Massachusetts,* who also took the opportunity of the rescue run to stage his own one-man air raid on damaged ships and a pier in the area.

The Palau Islands were then secured—American troops landed and took them—or enough of them to make airfield building possible.

Admiral Sherman's task group moved to Kossol roads, in the northern part of the atoll, becoming the first combat force to use this particular harbor. Captain Buracker was not very well pleased with it—from the standpoint of security. They were only five miles from the northern tip of Babelthuap Island, the largest island of the Palau atoll—and one literally swarming with Japanese troops. It had not been the intent to take the whole atoll at that time, but to take selective parts—it was a part of MacArthur's and Central Pacific's program of using what was needed and isolating the Japanese.

Also, Captain Buracker knew there were several Japanese submarines in the vicinity. None were found inside the anchorage, thank goodness, but some were certainly reported in the immediate vicinity.

Since it was so insecure a place, Admiral Sherman agreed that they would not stay there at night, the most dangerous time for a carrier. Instead they moved in to the shelter of the land for replenishment during the daylight hours, then moved out again at night, where they could zig-zag, and carry on their protective measures. If the Japanese attacked, they were much safer at sea than locked into the land.

They moved down to Ulithi atoll, which Admiral Halsey had selected as the most promising naval base in the area. Halsey wanted a big protected harbor as a place for replenishment, and a place where his men could go ashore for a little while between seagoing assignments. He had kept his eye on Ulithi for quite a while, and the fast carrier forces had bombed the islands three times in 1944. On the last strike Halsey had learned that the atoll was virtually deserted by the Japanese who had gone to Yap. They had considered the islands as of no use to anyone—not even worth defending. But the Americans were of a different view. Ulithi was occupied by the marines on September 23.

The Japanese did not even leave enough troops to make token opposition, and so the Americans were met by King Ueg of Ulithi and a handful of his followers, and welcomed to the strange, sandy atoll. Since it was so easy, the landing took only two days, and then Vice Admiral John H. Hoover took charge of the development of the forward base for the fleet. Falalop Island was selected for the air base, and Asor Island became the fleet base. A little hospital and a boat pool were quickly built by the Seabees on Sorlen, and MogMog was made into the fleet recreation base, with what the *Princeton* pilots were to declare as the longest bar in the world decorating the officers' club, going up under their noses.

Princeton arrived at Ulithi on the tail of a typhoon, and suffered through rough water even inside the lagoon, so rough that they feared to stay in, and so moved outside for two days to ride out the storm in deep water.

There was plenty of excitement, too. The Japanese had mined at least six of the little channels that ran between the islands of the atoll—showing that while they did not think it was worth much, they were not stupid either. A Minesweeper was sunk by one mine while sweeping Zowariyau channel on October 1. Nine men were killed and 14 were injured in this incident. While *Princeton* was riding out the typhoon outside, LCT-1052, not capable of standing up to a storm at deep sea the way *Princeton* was, was sunk off Asor island by the winds and waves. Two other LCT's were beached on October 3, and 79 small craft, brought to

Ulithi for staging in the coming landings, were actually sunk and lost.

Japanese submarines were hanging around the vicinity at this time, but instead of ganging up on the fighting ships, they contented themselves to reporting to Tokyo on the American build-up, and the admirals and generals of the Imperial Staff began to get a picture of the American effort. Yet they got a very imperfect picture, because the mass of the Philippine invasion that was building up was occurring in the south, under General MacArthur. There is good reason to believe that the Japanese never quite understood what they were up against in the Philippines—that counting the small vessels and the 700 major ships of the Seventh Fleet, and the Third Fleet and its support group, there were over a thousand vessels to contend with.

Indeed, the Japanese were very indefinite in their stocktaking of the Third Fleet itself, which was strengthened for the coming operations against the Japanese at Leyte.

Halsey had Third Fleet disposed as a Task Force, with a certain number of battleships and cruisers accompanying each of the groups of carriers. As for himself, he was riding in Task Group 38.2, which was commanded by Rear Admiral Gerald F. Bogan. Halsey's flagship, also a battleship assigned to general duty, was the *New Jersey*.

The next in command was Admiral Mitscher, who was riding in the carrier *Lexington,* which was in Admiral Sherman's Task Group 38.3 along with *Princeton*. The other carriers in that task group were *Essex* and *Langley,* and together they could mount 255 planes. But there was quite a difference between the big *Essex* class carriers, such as *Essex* herself, and the lighter carriers such as *Princeton* and *Langley*. The former carried nearly a hundred planes, the latter about a third as many. Yet multiplying everything by four—the number of task groups—it could be seen that Admiral Halsey's force packed a mighty wallop. He could put up a thousand planes in a day, and fly literally thousands of missions from his carriers.

Halsey's orders from Admiral Nimitz now called for

him to support the coming Leyte invasion strategically—and to Halsey that meant he was going to knock out the Japanese air strength in the Philippines, on Okinawa, and on Formosa so that the Japanese could not sink the American ships that pulled into Leyte Gulf to land their precious cargoes of troops and materiel.

That is why, when *Princeton* was at Ulithi, and Captain J.H. Hoskins reported to Admiral Sherman for duty, there was a certain amount of confusion. Captain Hoskins was to replace Captain Buracker, whose turn had come for "a blow" or some leave outside the fighting regions, after all his time at sea. But with the coming operations, which included fast strikes at the Japanese inner empire, neither Admiral Sherman nor Captain Buracker were entirely pleased with the idea of turning the ship over to a new commander. Not that Hoskins was not a good man—he had a long and distinguished record of his own. But all ships have their peculiarities, and it is one thing for a captain to take over, and another thing for a captain to take over on the eve of a vital fleet operation. So it was decided that Captain Hoskins would ride along with Captain Buracker as a passenger for the next few days, and then take command when there was a lull in the fighting and he had gotten his feet wet, so to speak.

On October 5, when the typhoon had blown by, Third Fleet rendezvoused at sea and began to head northwest. Action was in the offing.

The fleet headed for the Nansei Shoto Islands. The name of Okinawa was not then engraved on the hearts of Americans, and the names did not mean much more than those of Yahagi Shima and Kouri Shima. They were important, big islands—particularly Okinawa—and they contained thousands of Japanese and hundreds of airplanes—or they could at least. And that is why they were important.

They sortied from Ulithi, with Admiral Mitscher right there in the middle of the task group, and headed for the Nansei Shoto, in heavy seas and high winds that bounced the carriers up and down. The rendezvous came at dark, on October 7, about 375 miles west of the Marianas, and then they headed up for fuelling. All day long on October 8 the carriers and the battleships, the cruisers, and the destroyers, drank from the nine big oilers in the train. The decks were awash, the lines pulled and tugged, and there was danger that the fuelling mechanisms could be yanked right out of the ships by the pulling of the hoses. This had happened before—several times in the early days of the war, before the men of the carriers and those of the oilers got used to the exigencies of fuelling at sea in almost any kind of weather.

Halsey was a brilliant commander, and he did not telegraph his punches. While the fleet moved toward the Japanese empire, he sent a surface force up to the Bonin islands to bombard. It did its work. And yet, the Japanese were not really fooled. Admiral Toyoda, the chief of the Combined Japanese Fleet, had been expecting an attack on the Philippines for some time, and he was now making an inspection trip to see what he could expect in line of defense from this region. If he heard about the raid on Marcus, he did not pay much attention. Why should he? The raid was conducted by surface ships, and Admiral Toyoda knew very well that what he had to fear in this war was the carrier force of the Americans, which seemed to be growing endlessly.

As usual, the shooting at the Nansei Shoto started just before dawn. The planes of Task Force 38 flew 1,396 sorties, hit a submarine tender, 12 torpedo boats, a pair of midget submarines, four cargo ships, and alerted the Japanese naval air forces for the beginning of the SHO Plan. This action, in turn, meant that every operational plane would be devoted to destruction of the enemy wherever he might be met. The defense of the area depended on several commands. One of them was that of Vice Admiral Fukudome, who was in charge of Southern Kyushu, the Ryukyus, and Formosa. He had, in his Sixth Base Air

Force, 737 planes available. Then there was the Fifth Base Air Force and the army command in the Philippines. But the raids of September had hurt sorely, and there were fewer than 450 airplanes available to the Japanese here for defense. Still, some 1,200 planes was quite a lot, and besides that number, the Japanese could scrape up another 700 in Japan itself if the Admirals thought it was necessary. Nearly 2,000 planes available! It was a strong force, but it was much stronger on paper than in fact.

For example, only about 225 of the planes on Formosa were fighters, and when one goes to counter an attack, one does not want patrol bombers, observation planes, or even torpedo bombers. One wants fighters, and it is in the fighter quotient that the Japanese were particularly short. Altogether they could muster only about 500 fighters. Even to do this they would have to strip the six operational carriers of their planes.

Princeton played an important role in the attack. Six of her bombers made a low level attack against small ships and sampans between Okinawa and Yahagi, and at least three of the planes secured direct hits with their bombs. Two ships were seen to sink in these attacks, and when they were over, all the ships in the area were sinking or burning.

Another torpedo bomber, equipped with bombs, attacked a ship off Kouri island, and although the bomb missed, it was so close that it raised the entire afterend of the ship out of the water.

Five of *Princeton*'s fighters bombed and strafed two ships near Okinawa and three other fighters strafed and bombed another ship, using dive bomber tactics, coming down from 8,000 feet and then pulling out at 1,500 to 2,000 feet.

In its participation in this raid *Princeton* and her men were breaking new ground for the navy. Only one American carrier had ever come as close to Japan itself, and that was Admiral Halsey's *Hornet,* which had brought the B-25 medium bombers of General Jimmy Doolittle to within

600 miles of the Japanese islands before launching them, and that was more than two years earlier. It was a sign of the changing fortunes of the war that the Americans now dared walk into the Japanese empire itself. The nearest American air base was in the Marianas and for the Task Force to move in on Japan thus showed some part of the tremendous power that the carrier forces could raise on a few minutes' notice.

When Admiral Toyoda had finished the inspection of the Philippines defenses, he had moved on to Formosa to check on his air and naval defenses there. At Formosa he received news that was unheard-of—the American raid on Okinawa. Immediately he sensed the importance of this move. If the Americans could strike Okinawa, they could strike anywhere. They were, by Japanese terms, completely out of control.

At this time, the Japanese naval arm was still suffering from a shortage of planes, caused by the recent losses, and particularly the losses in the "Marianas Turkey Shoot." Worse than the shortage of planes was the shortage of pilots who could operate from carriers. Admiral Toyoda made an appraisal of the situation, but that is about all he could do. Communications between Formosa and his headquarters at Hiyoshi, outside Tokyo, were not of the best. In effect, not knowing precisely what was happening, Admiral Toyoda had to delegate his authority to Rear Admiral Kusaka, his chief of staff, who was in Japan. And Admiral Kusaka, feeling that something terrible was impending, did nothing.

There were, in fact, four SHO Plans for Japan. One showed what to do if the Americans landed in the Philippines. One considered the landings as coming on Formosa and the Ryukus. One set the action for Honshu-Kyushu—Japan itself—and the last was for defense of Hokkaido and the Kuriles. To be sure all these attacks had been considered by the Japanese. But this raid that was now coming on Formosa could be confusing—were the Americans heading for a landing in the Philippines or on Formosa? It could be either. Thus the fight would have to be first in the air, to knock out the American carrier force right now, before it could strike.

Here the weakness of the Japanese position is more than ever apparent, because the problem of the Japanese air forces could not be measured simply in numbers. For example, Japan had a special force for this operation, called the T Force, an "elite flying group" which boasted of its superiority. And yet, half of these pilots had only six months of training in flying over water. They simply were not adequately trained for the job at hand. A pilot of *Princeton*'s Air Group 23, with a year or more of training, and the careful carrier tactics built up for him, could simply fly rings around most of these inexperienced Japanese.

CHAPTER FIVE

Princeton *and the*
Formosa Air Battle

Admiral Halsey was now planning the first carrier strikes on Formosa, which would be carried out by Admiral Mitscher, who was known for taking his forces in close—perhaps 50 miles from the objective at times—so the men on ship could actually see the target. There the carriers would stay, steaming back and forth, watching for planes and submarine attacks, until the American planes had done their job. Air protection was provided by the CAP—Combat Air Patrol—and the anti-aircraft batteries; in addition, the force had its own surface fleet that was about as strong as anything the Japanese could possibly send against them.

If the Japanese did not yet know where the next strike was coming, at least they now knew that a strike was bound to come, and that it would represent the preliminaries to a new invasion. The American technique was now established. In the Central Pacific, the fast Carrier Task Force had hit a general region very heavily, breaking the airplane pipeline, and then the sea forces moved in carrying the invasion troops. This time some of the Japanese were not fooled at all. Admiral Fukudome, commanding land-based naval air squadrons, forecast quite accurately that Halsey's big air strike would be made against Formosa. Soon, on October 12, it began.

On that morning Task Force 38 arrived at launching

position, about 90 miles east of Formosa, before dawn. The force had been followed for hours by Japanese snoopers, but no Japanese plane attacked. Admiral Bogan's task group took care of the north end of the island, Admiral McCain's group took the south, and Admiral Davison's group took the important Takao area. *Princeton,* as part of Admiral Sherman's task group, was involved in the center of the big island.

Altogether it was a tremendous job of destruction, to Japanese shipping in the harbors and to the airfields and airplanes of the Japanese naval air arm. There were 1,378 sorties or flights that day from the carriers, and *Princeton* did her share, although that day her share was scarcely exciting. She was charged with flying Combat Air Patrol and anti-submarine patrol that first day. Her planes flew 83 sorties. In the morning one of the anti-submarine patrol planes found an enemy plane and helped shoot it down. It was a Betty, one of the big two-engine bombers. One fighter was damaged that day when it smashed into the barrier on landing, but not a pilot or a plane was lost. That was not the case with the fleet as a whole—the Formosan fields and ports were well protected by anti-aircraft and the Japanese flew up to meet the attackers. So the Americans lost 48 planes. But the Japanese losses numbered in the hundreds.

On the second day of the Formosa attack, *Princeton* was luckier. She was included in the striking force, having done her duty so well the day before. The Task Force was in position again at dawn, and the weather was good for air strikes, there was plenty of wind for launching and recovery, visibility was good, and cloud coverage helped the planes escape anti-aircraft and attackers.

The carriers began launching their planes before dawn, but *Princeton*'s planes came later. Strike No. 1 composed of eight fighters and seven torpedo bombers, took off in mid-morning for attack on the Asan Naval Base in the Pescadores Islands. The weather was terrible, the clouds hung gray and low over the sea, and the visibility at the target was very bad—rain and mist and cloud cover again. The bombers came and dropped their eggs on the base buildings, but they could not make very accurate estimates of the damage they did. The fighters strafed a small escort vessel and a medium-sized cargo ship in the harbor, but they could not make either ship burn.

At two o'clock in the afternoon, *Princeton*'s planes took off on a photographic mission for the task force. One camera-equipped fighter and two of her protective fighters were then launched to cover the beaches along the west coast of Formosa and particularly to check the airfields for damage, and possible hidden planes, which the Japanese camouflaged very cleverly and hid in revetments.

At the same time *Princeton* launched her second strike against the Japanese, eight fighters and four torpedo bombers which joined up with the planes of other carriers. The fighters hit Kagi airfield and the bombers went after a power plant at Jintsugetsutan. The bomber strike was spectacularly effective. One plane scored a direct hit on a big building. As for the fighters, they found some 20 Japanese planes on the ground at Kagi airfield and strafed them thoroughly, but could not make any of them burn. One division of *Princeton* fighters was luckier—it found a flight of three Japanese planes low in the air, off the west coat of Formosa. They swooped down on the Japanese, and shot down all three of them. And the Combat Air Patrol, flying its boring circles, was rewarded with one Japanese snooper, which it shot down.

October 13 was a tough day for the Carrier Task Force, however. The opposition was severe. The reason was that the Japanese had seen what was happening and decided to commit their strength to this battle and knock out the American carriers if they could. They used the same old tactics, coming in at evening. The carrier *Franklin* had quite an adventure that evening. Four Bettys came in, concealed by clouds and flying so low they were not found by the radar in the circling of American planes that were landing that evening. The Bettys divided, to attack, and came in with their torpedoes. One was shot down by a fighter, another was shot down by anti-aircraft fire. A third Betty came so close to drop his torpedo, that he had to fly *up* to clear the *Franklin*—and as he flew over he was shot down. The torpedo came hissing in through the water, and Captain J.M. Shoemaker just barely saved his ship by ordering full speed astern. The carrier responded, shuddering, and the slowing of her movement was just enough to make the torpedo miss.

Then in came a fourth Betty, flying across the stern, and dropping his torpedo low. It sizzled in, and passed just beneath the ship's fantail. Really a close one! As for the Betty, it caught a burst of anti-aircraft fire and began to blaze, then crashed into the carrier's flight deck and slid across it, trailing flames—and then lurched completely overboard, leaving a haze of smoke on the deck behind.

Franklin was not a casualty, but another ship was badly hit that day. She was the heavy cruiser *Canberra*, which took a torpedo as dusk settled over the fleet. The Japanese bombers were very effective that day with their evening attack and low flying technique, and eight of them came in on *Canberra*, totally undetected by the American radar. Six planes were shot down, but one sent a torpedo into *Canberra* blowing a huge hole in the side of the ship and killing 23 men. Flames began to spurt into the air. In a few moments the ship stopped. Water rushed into the engine and firerooms, and it seemed that she would have to be sunk because she could not get home by herself.

But Admiral Halsey was not about to lose a good ship if he could save her, so he decided to brave the growing wrath of the Japanese and establish a towing mission which would take *Canberra* back to Ulithi. It was a dangerous plan, because a crippled ship is always an easy target for enemy bombers. And Halsey would have to risk other ship carriers, cruisers, and destroyers, to protect the crippled *Canberra*. But he was a brave and determined commander, and that was what he was going to do.

The cruiser *Wichita* set about towing the *Canberra*, and

shortly after midnight the force was moving again, away from the Japanese.

But towing was not all of it. Halsey decided that he would strike Formosa again on October 14, although it had previously been planned that the Task Force would move away from the island for refueling. But Halsey had to protect the slow-moving *Canberra* as much as he could, so another strike was in order.

Princeton was deeply involved that next day. Along with planes from *Essex*, eight fighters loaded with one-hundred-pound bombs set out for an airfield north of Taichu and plastered it early in the morning. They destroyed three single-engine planes and three biplanes by strafing, and damaged others with their bombs.

The Japanese had called up their strongest forces from the homeland, including the planes of their carriers in the Sea of Japan, and all that day enemy planes swarmed around *Princeton* and other ships of the fleet. In addition to the attacks against Japanese installations the pilots were busy defending their ships this day. During the morning the planes managed to keep all the Japanese away from the formation. In the afternoon the Japanese grew more aggressive and *Princeton* fired on one plane that came very close. Later in the afternoon, the Combat Air Patrol was augmented by another three planes because there were so many Japanese around. At 3:30 in the afternoon, a Zero was singled out and shot down. The other Japanese were kept away by the fighters, and the air was soon clear of them. But the Japanese did not give up. They came back around 5:50 in the evening, as the day grew longer, with their torpedo planes. *Princeton* shot down two with her anti-aircraft fire, and kept shooting for half an hour at others that tried to come in. Again the Japanese were coming in low, virtually skimming the water, for they had learned that the only way to get in among the American ships was to avoid that telltale radar. They used another trick—window—which was a technique of dropping aluminum foil from their planes. The foil fell slowly to the water, confusing the radar screens, which was just what the Japanese wanted. Buy by far the most effective method they used was the skimming method, when they flew at less than fifty feet above the waves all the way in. That afternoon, no one hurt *Princeton,* but one Japanese plane did crash into the fantail of the cruiser *Renos.* It did some damage.

Then a large group of Japanese planes was picked up on the radar screen, coming in from the northeast. The gunners patted the barrels of their guns, or fidgeted in their seats, waiting. In the combat information center, the men watched the blips on the radar screen. In the air, two divisions (six planes) of the air patrol were vectored out and told to find the blips and knock them down if they were Japanese.

The air patrol moved out. Soon they came upon 16 Japanese planes, 40 miles away from the ship and moving in. They were flying at 700 feet in a diamond formation when the Americans spotted them and swooped down. The Japanese broke formation, then, and most of them tried to head for the clouds. But the fast American fighters were on them, swooping and shooting, and in a few minutes they brought down 13 of the 16 Japanese planes and furiously pursued the others until they lost them in the growing cloud cover.

But the Japanese were not finished for the day. They were sending out their torpedo bombers as dusk began to fall, in their typical maneuver to hit the Americans at their weakest hour of the day—when they were recovering planes and when visibility was not generally very good.

Some dozen torpedo bombers moved against Admiral McCain's task group, which was operating on the northern end of the island, and a torpedo smashed into the side of *Houston,* one of the Force's light cruisers. Almost immediately the lights went out and all power was lost. The lower spaces began to flood, and it looked so bad for the ship that destroyers began to cluster around to take off the crew. Captain W.W. Behrens asked for reports from his damage control parties and they were so negative that he informed Admiral McCain that he was about to order the ship abandoned. The destroyers came in and they began to take off men. But then Captain Behrens had more encouraging reports from his officers. He decided to try to save the ship.

In came the cruiser *Boston* to give him a tow.

Now Admiral Halsey had two crippled ships on his hands. In the exigencies of battle, anyone would have forgiven him for abandoning both of them, taking off all the men and sinking them. Because on the next day he was supposed to move, and in the next few days he was supposed to neutralize the Philippine airfields for the beginning of the invasion at Leyte. Halsey talked it over with his staff and decided that he could do both jobs—hit the airfields and bring home the stricken ships. A special Task Force, including the cruisers *Santa Fe, Birmingham,* and *Mobile,* and light carriers *Cowpens* and *Cabot,* was detached to guard the cripples and see them back to the safety of the base at Ulithi.

Seeing the cripples, Japanese pilots gained a strange impression of what they had accomplished in this battle of the Formosan air and water. It must be remembered that the Japanese had made this a special effort, and, as they went out to fight, the Japanese pilots were abjured to kill the Americans and knock them away from the doors of the empire. It was deemed essential that the American fleet be stopped here, and the Japanese knew they were using their fullest resources of air power to stop the Americans. So it was not too difficult for them and some of their officers to believe that they actually had done what they were expected to do. Japanese planes flying above the crippled *Houston* and *Canberra* first thought they were sinking, then thought they had sunk, and then identified them as other ships. So it was not long, on the afternoon of October 14, before Admiral Toyoda, the commander of the Japanese fleet, believed that the Americans were retiring in defeat. Perhaps he had expected an American invasion of

Formosa by this fleet. Actually Halsey had done exactly what he wanted to do—maybe more. But the Japanese thought they had beaten him. Actually Halsey and the Third Fleet were moving back to the Philippines to undertake their next operation.

On October 15 and 16 the Japanese threw every plane they could muster into the battle against the Third Fleet. The carriers—or some of them—spent these days with their Combat Air Patrols doing much of the work, fighting off the Japanese. It was estimated that nearly a thousand Japanese planes attacked in these days, and that the Task Force fought them off with practically no ship damage and relatively few planes lost or pilots killed.

The movement of the special Task Force that protected the two hurt cruisers was very slow. The Force had to surround the cruisers, and circle them to give protection against attacking Japanese planes. They did so and the two light carriers put planes up to knock down more Japanese.

Admiral Toyoda ordered Admiral Fukudome to destroy the "remnants" of the American fleet, and Fukudome tried to do so. But he soon learned how the Americans could fight. He attacked Admiral Davison's task group with some ninety planes in one wave—and twenty of them were shot down, the rest scurried home. On October 15 three waves of Japanese planes tried to "get" the cruisers that were damaged—and all three waves failed. The carrier *Franklin* was hit that day, when one bomber managed to put a bomb on the corner of the deck elevator. Three men were killed and a dozen were wounded.

The next day, October 16, the Japanese made an even more furious attempt to knock out the crippled warships. Nearly a hundred planes came after them, and then, for some unknown reason, turned back before they found them. Then just after noon, 107 Japanese planes found the Force at the entrance to Luzon strait and attacked. Fighters shot down nearly fifty of them, but one torpedo plane got through, and put another torpedo into *Houston*.

Wham! went the explosion.

Twenty men were blown overboard.

The hangar hatch went up like the lid of a garbage can when a boy puts a firecracker inside.

Bulkheads, inside the ship, collapsed and leaks developed below the waterline.

Admiral DuBose, the commander of the Force, came alongside in *Santa Fe*.

"Is your case hopeless?" he asked through the megaphone.

"Not hopeless, grave," said Captain Behrens.

The fleet tug *Pawnee* came along.

"WE'LL STAND BY YOU," was her message.

And stand by they did. So did the whole fleet.

The plane that had done the damage flew alongside the *Houston* as if in triumph. But that was the pilot's last. The anti-aircraft gunners shot him down. And then the gunners of *Santa Fe* unleashed their fury on another Japanese plane that tried to torpedo their ship—and shot it completely in two to see it fall just in front of the ship's bow.

Meanwhile strange events were occurring in Japan. The fliers who returned from their missions made wild reports of the damages they were inflicting on the American fleet, and each pilot seemed eager to outdo his fellows in the tales he told. Soon Radio Tokyo was claiming a major victory over the Americans and telling the world that Halsey was limping home with a handful of ships from his once proud fleet.

Halsey laughed when he heard what Radio Tokyo was saying, but not so loudly that he failed to take advantage of the Japanese near-sightedness. He stationed Task Group 38.3—*Princeton*'s group—between the crippled ships and Japan, in the hope that the Japanese would send out their navy to clean up the "cripples." In fact, the Japanese did just that.

Vice Admiral Shima was ordered to take three cruisers and three destroyers, and move out from the Inland Sea to destroy the ships that were limping home. He set out on the morning of October 15, full of hope, and propaganda. But on the morning of October 16, when refueling his destroyers, Admiral Shima's force was suddenly attacked by two planes from the carrier *Bunker Hill*, and he soon learned that the Americans had set a trap for him. So *Princeton*'s planes did not get their chance that day at the enemy fleet. And then Shima learned that half a dozen carriers were operating in the area, and the propaganda barrage, at least with the admirals, began to slow down. The Japanese began to learn what had happened to them and their airplanes in the battle of Formosa; what had happened was disaster; the Island of Formosa and the Philippine Islands had virtually been stripped of operational aircraft on the eve of the American attack on Leyte. As for the Americans, they had lost 89 planes in the whole operation, and the Japanese had lost nearly ten times as many.

In this battle the Japanese showed an awesome ability to fool themselves. They claimed to have sunk eleven carriers, two battleships, three cruisers, and one destroyer, and to have damaged eight more carriers, two battleships, four cruisers, and a destroyer. Radio Tokyo made these claims with a straight face, and finally goaded Admiral Halsey into reporting that he was "retiring" toward the enemy.

It was unusual for Admiral Chester Nimitz to make any statements at a time like this, but he could see that the Japanese story, if left to stand alone, might be convincing to some Americans, so he released the message that Halsey was retiring toward the enemy, having salvaged all the Third Fleet ships reported sunk by the Japanese.

And it was strictly true. Halsey was on the loose again, smashing the Japanese in and around the Philippines. The ships that had been hurt, *Canberra* and *Houston*, were steaming steadily, if slowly, toward safety and would be repaired.

And the Japanese air power in and around the Philippines had been blasted to little bits. It was a tremendous victory for the planes of *Princeton* and the other carriers.

CHAPTER SIX

The Bomb

Princeton and the other units of the fast Carrier Task Force moved. They fueled. They steamed to a point off Luzon Island, and from there made strikes against the Japanese airfields, as the American landing forces made ready to assault the beaches of Leyte Island to the south. After some preliminary attacks the main landings were made in Leyte Gulf on October 20, using some 700 ships in the operation.

General MacArthur made a landing that day, too. He came from the cruiser *Nashville* off the beach, and got into a barge and was taken to Philippine soil, which he had left early in 1942. He waded knee-deep in water to the beach, and then he made a speech.

"People of the Philippines," he said, "I have returned."

He was keeping the promise he had made to them when he was driven from Corregidor in those desperate days when the war seemed to be going all Japan's way.

Princeton and the other carriers, meanwhile, were fueling and fighting, hitting those Japanese airfields in the north. *Princeton*'s planes attacked the airfields of the southern islands on October 21. The next day was spent largely in standing by, waiting to see if the planes would be needed to strike any special areas. They were not needed that day. On October 23, *Princeton* made more air strikes on Japanese fields.

Meanwhile, many things were happening that were to affect the future of the fast carriers, and of *Princeton* in particular. The Japanese fleet had decided to make the Leyte Gulf landings a major naval battle. Four different Japanese forces were at sea on October 23, preparing to close in on Leyte and destroy the landing forces that were already well ashore and established on the beaches. *Princeton* was ranging off the beach, 150 miles from Manila, with the task group during the night of the 23rd and early hours of October 24.

From various sources, including the two submarines which attacked Admiral Kurita's main force that was coming through the Palawan passage, Admiral Halsey learned of the movements of the Japanese fleet, and prepared on October 24 to smash away at that fleet. *Princeton* and the other ships of the task group, including *Lexington*, the flagship of Admiral Mitscher, moved to the east of the Polillo Islands, to cover the west coast of Luzon, and the other task groups spread out in other areas to be sure they could manage the Japanese.

On the flagship of the Third Fleet, the battleship *New Jersey*, Halsey and his chief of staff, Rear Admiral Robert B. Carney, were in constant discussion of the plans of the Japanese. These could not be known by the Americans, in detail, but it was apparent to Carney and Halsey that something big was moving that day.

It was hard to believe. "Viewed from our standpoint the hazards of such counter measures seemed to be so great that it was difficult to believe the Japanese would undertake them," said Carney. "But by the night of the 23rd it was apparent that something on a grand scale was underfoot and the decision was made to move in close to the east coast of the Philippines to project reinforced searches across the Philippines into the South China sea to find out just what was going on."

The men of *Princeton*, and *Essex*, and the other carriers

of the task group were very tired by this time. They had been fighting since October 10 without a letup. But when the chips seemed to be down, as they did this night, that situation did not make any difference. The men of the fighting fleet made ready to fight again the next morning.

On the night of the 23rd, Task Group 38.3 moved into the little bight of Luzon where Polillo was located. The group consisted that day of the flagship *Essex,* a fleet carrier, with Rear Admiral Sherman aboard; and fleet carrier *Lexington,* with Vice Admiral Mitscher aboard.

Then came *Princeton,* and *Langley,* the two light carriers; two battleships, the *Massachusetts* and *South Dakota,* four cruisers, the *Santa Fe, Mobile, Birmingham,* and *Reno;* and thirteen destroyers: the *Porterfield, C.K. Bronson, Cotten, Dortch, Gatling, Healy, Callaghan, Cassin Young, Irwin, Preston, Laws, Longshaw,* and *Morrison.*

By daybreak the task group had placed itself about 60 miles east of Polillo, and was waiting for dawn. Throughout the night, Japanese snoopers kept appearing around the task group. At about 2:30 in the morning, one was shot down, but that did not prevent the Japanese from coming back. By five o'clock in the morning, no fewer than five snoopers were seen on the screens of the task group.

Now there was a reason for this. The Japanese knew that their own forces were making ready to come through to attack the Americans on the morning of October 25. Ships were at sea in the four different forces. First was Admiral Kurita's force of battleships and cruisers and destroyers. It had set out from the Singapore area, and was heading into the Sibuyan Sea that cuts between the Philippine Islands. Admiral Kurita would move around, through the San Bernardino strait, and would then make his Force become the northern half of a pincer, designed to catch the Americans in Leyte Gulf in the middle. The southern half of the pincer was to be made up of two smaller Japanese forces, one led by Admiral Nishimura, which had also sailed from Singapore, and one led by Admiral Shima, who had chased the American "remnants" a few days before, until he learned that they were not remnants at all, but a sturdy fleet, and then had moved back into the Formosa area. These two admirals were to come around from the south, through the Sulu Sea, and make the southern or bottom half of the pincers.

To support them, and draw away Admiral Halsey and the Third Fleet with its carriers and fast battleships, the Japanese had sent down Admiral Jisaburo Ozawa from Japan, with a fleet of carriers, battleships, and cruisers. It sounded as though Ozawa had a fierce and fearsome fleet, but the fact was that his carriers had virtually no aircraft on them, because the planes had been stripped and sent to Formosa to engage in the awesome battle described earlier. He was coming down the east coast of the Philippines from the north, and so close that he might even run into part of Halsey's fleet, but as yet—in the early hours of October 24—the Americans knew only of "milling around" and had no specific ideas of the Japanese plan or strengths.

For the morning to come, the orders of the task group were to put up reinforced search teams, to move west of Luzon, to a distance of 300 miles, and the carriers began launching before dawn, which was to come with sunrise at 6:46 in the morning.

The men of *Princeton* were moving then. At 5:20 the ship went to general quarters, which meant everyone on the alert and at action stations. Then at 6:10, the launchings began, first from *Essex* and *Lexington*. These ships put up fighters and bombers to cover sectors of the compass from 245 degrees to 295 degrees (easterly) out to 300 miles. They would include the Sibuyan Sea and the area around Mindoro where the Japanese fleet elements that had been attacked in Palawan passage (Kurita's force) were supposed to be.

At the same time, *Langley* launched the anti-submarine patrol, which was her special duty that morning, and the anti-snooper patrol, designed to keep those bothersome Japanese observation planes out of the area. *Langley* also put up a four-plane Combat Air Patrol, while *Essex* launched a 20-plane fighter sweep to move against the airfields around Manila. *Princeton*'s task at the moment was to put up two divisions of fighters, or eight fighters in all. These would form an important part of the Combat Air Patrol.

The morning began with gusto. Enemy snoopers were still around the area, and by 7:50 *Princeton*'s air patrol planes had shot down two of them, and *Langley*'s patrol planes had shot down two more.

Now two other planes of the group were sent out as communications links, and stationed 100 and 200 miles out, to relay the contact reports of the search planes that were looking for the Japanese fleet. The decks of the carriers, *Princeton*, and the others, were filled with planes just waiting for the word from the searchers so the strikes against the enemy could be launched.

No search to the north or east of Luzon was ordered, and this omission was to prove important later in the day. Also the use of so many planes from this task group left the Combat Air Patrol short, which Admiral Sherman noted, but could do nothing about. That fact, too, was to play a role in the events of the next few hours.

Aboard the *Princeton*, plans were made by Captain Buracker for a long, hard day. He expected that the men and officers would spend most of the day at General Quarters, and breakfast was served that morning at battle stations. Other preparations were made for the aerial attacks that the men of *Princeton* fully expected to develop. The Japanese had been very quiet, with their snoopers out high and wide, and the Captain and his crew were ready for what might come. For one thing, fire hoses were led out on the flight and hangar decks, so that if the enemy came in, they would be ready for what he might deliver.

At 7:50 that morning, it became apparent that *Princeton* and the other ships of the task group were in for trouble from the Japanese. On the radar screen the blips began to show up, and soon the operators were counting 40 to 50 Japanese planes, stacked up in the air and coming toward them—stacked, meaning coming in at various altitudes, from 25,000 feet down to the deck level. Just then they were out to the west, and 75 miles away. *Princeton*'s Combat Air Patrol was vectored out to intercept, and Admiral Sherman ordered all carriers to launch more fighters. Soon Princeton had 12 more fighters in the air, and the other ships were putting up more fighters too. The original air patrol began to intercept the enemy about 50 miles from the formation, and were joined by fighters from other carriers. Soon, a general air fight began, and at the same time search planes found the Japanese fleet, and reported sighting four battleships, eight cruisers, and a number of escorts heading into the Sibuyan Sea from south of the island of Mindoro.

Within a few minutes, a third large enemy air raid appeared on the screens of the task group, bearing 240 degrees, and 60 miles away. So *Lexington* launched her remaining 12 fighters to protect the whole group. Admiral Sherman had planned to send off the air strike, but now he did not have enough fighters to do so. It had to be delayed. Also, with the Japanese coming in so fast, Admiral Sherman had to begin radical maneuvers to avoid the enemy, and this meant he could not keep his carriers headed up into the wind.

Sherman led the force into the rain squalls that dotted the sea this morning, moving from one into another, while the enemy was about, and coming out to the edge only to launch planes or land them.

The battle began, and in the melee the radar screen became completely confused with the large number of friendly and enemy aircraft mixed together as blips. The big one was raid No. 3, a group of about 50 planes divided evenly among dive bombers, torpedo planes, and fighters. From Admiral Sherman's own flagship came the leader of this fight, Commander David McCampbell, the leader of the *Essex* air group. Here is his story of the battle that morning:

"I was spotted on the catapult, the number one spot for

a strike on the Sibuyan sea unit, the five battleship unit, and we got word of this raid coming in. It had already closed to about 45 miles, and so I was launched in a scramble. In other words we scrambled all the fighters available at that particular time . . . we got seven off.

"Anyway we intercepted them about 30 miles from our own ships. They had altitude on us at the time, about the time we sighted them they started to turn to the left, apparently searching or having overshot the position they thought we were in. We never figured out why they turned left . . ."

Commander McCampbell motioned to his wingman, Lt. (jg) Rushing, and they led the seven-fighter force in against the 50 or 60 of the enemy who were milling about at this time. The Japanese bombers were diving into the overcast to escape.

McCampbell swiftly laid out his strategy. He and the first combat team would start at the top and work down on the planes stacked at various altitudes. The second combat team was to hit the stragglers and the bombers that were slower than the fighters.

So they went in.

Then there was a mixup in communications. They shifted channels, and some of the men did not get the message. They did not hear McCampbell's orders for that reason, and in a few moments, instead of having four fighters to work with, McCampbell found himself alone except for Lt. Rushing. Five of the fighters went down after those bombers that seemed to be sitting, so welcoming, below.

No one could criticize those pilots, they had not heard the latest instructions, and off they went, guns chattering, to knock down a dozen of the Japanese bombers.

But now McCampbell and his wingman found themselves face to face with some 40 Japanese fighters. The Japanese saw that McCampbell had altitude on them, and they undoubtedly guessed that there were dozens of fighters behind him, because they went suddenly into a big defensive Luberry circle—like a giant ferris wheel, a technique in which each plane protected the rear of the one ahead of it.

When they were in such a formation, McCampbell had better sense than to take them on—it might have been suicidal to attack so many planes so stoutly defended. But he was above them, so all he had to do was circle around the formation, on top of it, watch, and wait for the Japanese to make a move. They could not get anywhere, circling as they were. They had to come out of it sometime or run out of gas.

McCampbell waited. He called Rushing on the radio and said he thought the Japanese would run out of gas pretty soon—or at least get to the critical point. This group, he estimated, had come from Manila, and could not have too much fuel left. They would have to act soon. He had the advantage because his planes had plenty of gas.

The Japs would have to head somewhere soon, he said comfortingly. That's when they would get them. There was no question in his mind of running away or crying for help, against 40 Japanese fighters. He was just waiting for a chance to get at them.

It was fifteen minutes before the chance began to develop. Infuriatingly, the Japanese circled lazily, and circled again. But finally, at the end of those fifteen minutes, the Japanese leader pulled out of the Luberry, and turned north, to head for Manila.

Now, indeed, McCampbell did call for help, because he was afraid the Japanese would get away. Time after time he spoke into his microphone, asking someone, anyone, to come and help him shoot down these Japanese. For the next hour and a half he fought and yelled, and finally got one pilot—one of the five who had gone down after the bombers—to come up and help them. He could not understand why the *Essex* or the *Princeton* or one of the other carriers did not help. But there was a reason. Shortly after he took off, another raid had moved in on the ships, and they had to put up the remainder of their fighters to fight that one off. The planes were busy—there were just too many Japanese in the air to make it possible for the carriers to give McCampbell what he needed.

By this time the bombers were scattered or shot down. The five men of McCampbell's force had done a good job. And of course, as far as the Japanese commander of fighters was concerned, his reason for being in this dangerous area was gone—he had lost contact with the bombers he was supposed to protect.

In view of the fierce reputation of the Japanese in their Zero fighters, it seems odd that 40 Japanese would flee from a pair of Americans. But there were reasons. First of these: the superiority of the F6F fighter over the Japanese Zero in speed and maneuverability, and particularly in armor. When the war began, the Japanese undoubtedly had the superior fighter in their Zero, or Zeke, but Admiral Nimitz and his air commanders soon saw what they were up against and ordered the design of a new fighter, to match the Japanese product. More than that, it outmatched it, if for no other reason than armament. The Japanese had sacrificed pilot safety for speed and turning radius. The sacrifice was to play hob with the Japanese air force and had already at the "Marianas Turkey Shoot" and here in the Philippines. The Japanese were cut down to a handful of experienced pilots, and many of these were now very nervous; their planes often malfunctioned, and they simply did not represent the first class Japanese fliers; obviously expecting that McCampbell was supported by dozens of other planes, the Japanese headed home.

McCampbell and Rushing followed them, taking it easy, and waiting until someone climbed a little high, or dragged a little behind. When one of the Japanese slipped out of the tight formation, they were on him in a moment.

The Japanese scissored—they moved up and down and weaved at the same time—making a very elusive target. If McCampbell and Rushing committed themselves against the formation, it would be easy for the Japanese to slide away suddenly, and then the pair would find themselves under the enemy guns.

But McCampbell was patient. He waited, and because he was so careful, the Japanese did not get a single shot at him or at Rushing.

"During the next hour or so we followed the formation of weaving fighters, taking advantage of every opportunity to knock down those who attempted to climb to our altitude, scissored, went outside, straggled, or they became too eager and came to us singly. In all we made 18 to 20 passes, being very careful not to expose ourselves, and to conserve ammunition by withholding fire until within very close range."

So they fought. Commander McCampbell knocked down nine Japanese planes. Lieutenant Rushing knocked down six. There were undoubtedly more, because McCampbell and Rushing saw probables. They would fire, the Japanese plane would slide out of formation and begin to slip off on one wing, smoking. But he would dive into a cloud, or pull away from the formation, and they had no time to go down and track.

They followed and followed, growing lower on gasoline themselves—for they still had to go home to the carrier. And then the issue was decided for them because they ran out of ammunition, just as the Japanese formation began to dive down into the clouds, apparently reaching the vicinity of its bases. So they turned, and headed homeward. Then they got back to the carrier group, Admiral Sherman had the deck of *Essex* ready for a take off of the air strike he was so eager to make, and there was no place on his own carrier for McCampbell to land. He circled, and went to *Langley,* which took him aboard. He had exactly six gallons of gasoline left in his tanks.

Meanwhile the Combat Air Patrol of *Princeton* was doing a good job. The fighters had gone up and they began sending down Japanese planes from that second raid, Bettys and Judys and fighter planes.

As to the rest of the task group planes, their job had been to send the fighter sweep over Manila, send air searches out three-hundred miles to look for the Japanese fleet, and to furnish the Combat Air Patrol. Here is how the fighter sweep went as related in the records of *Essex'* air group. (*Princeton's* records of that day were lost.)

The fighters took off just before dawn to move over southwest Luzon and the China Sea approaches.

On their way out, flying near a Japanese airfield, one fighter reported a "bogey," and that gave him the right to go after it. He headed in and quickly slid behind the two-engined Japanese plane, for a flat rear approach. [The plane did not have a stinger or tail gun or turret.] He continued to circle with the Japanese plane until he closed in on it, and then he opened fire. One engine and one wing tank caught fire, and the Lily started into a dive and dove headlong into the ground.

Next, out in the sea, west of Luzon, the fighters encountered a lonely Japanese fighting ship, either a light cruiser or a destroyer. [There were several lone ships at sea that day in the region.] By this time, the bombers had already dropped their bombs, but the fighters had not dropped theirs, so the commander of the air group put the bombers ahead to fly "fighter cover" for the fighters, and the bombers went in and strafed the ship, while the fighters moved off to bomb. (Here was a very good indication of the versatility of the American fighting planes of the third year of the war.)

The fighters came in low in a glide bombing attack, through intense anti-aircraft fire, scoring one hit and three near misses—slowing down the ship and leaving it streaming oil.

On the way home Ensign Self discovered two Zeroes just taking off from their airfield, and notified his division leader. He then did a wingover, and fired full into the cockpit of one Zero. The Zero fell back to earth, ground looped off its right wing, nosed, breaking off the left wing, and burst into flames. The American kept on shooting. The pilot of the Japanese plane rose up in the cockpit and fell back again, hit.

Another pilot went after the second Zero, and hit it in

the engine, starting a fire. The Zero was at 300 feet then, and the pilot bailed out, but his parachute was just beginning to blossom when he hit the ground. The plane turned off to the right and went into a long gliding turn, then crashed.

Another of the task group's search teams was sent to the north nearer the Manila area. On the way out toward the search area, not far from the carriers the searchers spotted a Japanese snooper plane, and realized it was important that it be shot down. So one fighter jettisoned his bomb to give him extra speed, moved in on the stern of the Japanese plane, and began firing. The Japanese plane burst into flames, did a wingover, and dove into the sea.

About an hour later, on the cross leg of the triangular search pattern, the leader of the fighter, Lt. (jg) Symmes, spotted two Bettys and another plane at a thousand feet, flying together. When the Japanese looked up and saw the Americans, they divided and took evasive action. But the Americans were too quick for them, and in a few moments one Japanese plane made the mistake of turning right into the American formation, and stood up on one wing. The Americans marvelled at the right turning radius of this particular Japanese plane—which they called an Irving—but that did not prevent one pilot from taking after the Japanese, shooting, and sending him into a vertical dive that carried the two-engined plane down into the water.

One of the two Bettys in the group of planes was assigned to Lt. (jg) Mellon, who went in high from the side and shot at the cockpit, getting hits and starting a fire in the starboard engine. The Japanese pilot was good—he put the plane into a long glide and took it down for an almost perfect landing. But his canopy jammed, or he was hit, for the plane gurgled beneath the water. There were no survivors.

Lt. (jg) Stime went after the second Betty, diving in from four o'clock, opening fire when very close to the plane. The starboard engine began to smoke, and then to burn. The pilot tried to do what his companion had done, but the plane fell off on one wing, turned a fast cartwheel, the right wing broke off, and the fuselage plummeted into the water.

On this same search mission, the planes saw a damaged *Aoba* class cruiser (it was the *Aoba* which had been torpedoed while on a supply mission in Manila bay.) They also attacked other planes on the ground and in the air, and they suffered a minor casualty. One bomber's cowling came loose during a strafing run, and the pilot headed home, escorted by a fighter plane. He made it back safely.

Meanwhile, a mixed group of fighters and bombers from the carrier force flew out to try to find the enemy in the Sibuyan Sea. At 0849, the ships were found just off Mindoro island. They had been seen earlier, by other ships of Admiral Halsey's fleet, the first report coming in at 0810, from search planes of Task Group 38.2 led by Admiral Bogan. They were battleships, cruisers, and destroyers, said the report.

Admiral Halsey had sprung to action. He had intercepted that report before it came to him through normal channels, and he put out several urgent dispatches. Admiral McCain had been sent off to Ulithi to provision his ships and take on some new planes after the hard fighting of the last few days. His task group was called back to action. Then Halsey sent an urgent message to Admiral Sherman and to Admiral Davison, asking them to begin attacking the Japanese fleet.

Davison's group could do so. They began attacking at 0905 that morning, and hit a battleship, a cruiser, and several destroyers. They also found a small force (Nishimura's) which was streaming along in the southern waters of the Sulu Sea, but they decided (and so did Halsey) to leave that force to the mercies of Admiral Kinkaid and his Seventh Fleet, which had its own force of escort carriers, and to concentrate on the powerful group of battleships and cruisers—including the two biggest battleships in the world, the *Yamato* and the *Musashi*.

But the Japanese had their own plan for that day, and it called for the maximum use of their air power to knock out the task groups. Thus, more than 1,000 planes swarmed around the Task Group 38.3 in which *Princeton* rode. All around Admiral Sherman came reports of splashing Japanese planes, and then the combat controllers gave one order— "Hey Rube"—an old show business call for help. What it meant to the fighters of the task group out over the Manila was to come home and come home quickly and they did so smashing Japanese planes on the ground and in the air as they came.

From 7:50 in the morning on, the *Princeton* had been busy. Her fighters were put in the air, division by division, to intercept the Japanese, and they did so. First one group of Japanese and then another were stopped cold by *Princeton* and her companion carriers. When the second group of fighters came in, fifteen miles behind the first, the *Princeton*'s planes were out to meet these 30 planes, and turn them back. They turned to the northwest, and met fighters of the *Lexington* too. And two divisions of fighters from *Princeton* were vectored out to help, and got into the action. In those actions alone the planes of *Princeton* showed how good they were, they shot down 34 Japanese airplanes, with a loss of one *Princeton* fighter.

Between eight and nine o'clock in the morning, the task group maneuvered to take advantage of the rain squalls, and there was no attack—at least not a successful attack delivered on any of the ships.

When the word came in that the Japanese fleet was out, and that four battleships, eight cruisers and some 13 destroyers had been spotted off Mindoro, plans were made to launch the strike of fighters and bombers, which would include eight fighters and nine torpedo planes from *Princeton*. It could not be done immediately; the bombers were available and were spotted on deck, but *Princeton*'s fighters had been committed to the general defense, and it would be necessary to launch the bombers, then clear the decks and land the fighters, service them, and put them in the air once again. The torpedo planes were already loaded and armed, and fully gassed, including auxiliary wing tanks to carry them the long distance to the enemy and give them adequate shooting time.

At 8:45 that morning the second enemy attack on the task group was broken up completely and orders were received from Admiral Sherman to recover and reservice enough fighters to accompany the torpedo planes in the attack group. At the time, there were some enemy aircraft on the screen, some in the north, some in the west, and some in the south, but none of them were within 20 or 25 miles and they were not regarded as dangerous. Then there was one bogey showing—about 15 miles ahead of the formation. Planes were vectored out to find it and bring it down.

At 9:00 all the carriers were heading into the wind. The region was quiet and they were recovering the planes they had sent out three hours before, fighters low on gasoline, and ammunition. The formation was steering a course 065 degrees—northeast—and the speed was 24 knots which was excellent for flight operations.

The Combat Air Patrol and anti-submarine patrol planes were about ready to land, low on gasoline and moving into the pattern above the *Princeton*. Six of the loaded torpedo bombers, then, were moved to the hangar deck and spotted in a fore and aft line on the part side of the ship. Then *Princeton* began recovering her fighters. First the first eight fighters of the Combat Air Patrol which had been up longest came down. Then came two more fighters which had been scrambled at the alert in the early morning. Two more circled overhead, ready to land but held up because *Essex* reported a bogey about six miles out. Captain Buracker was eager to land his planes and check them, for he needed at least eight fighters to accompany his share of the strike on the Japanese in the Sibuyan Sea. But there was nothing to be done except wait—for there was a standing rule that when a bogey was reported close in, a carrier was very cautious. The worst possible time to get caught was when the decks were filled with planes, or when you were landing them and could not fight back.

About ten minutes after nine the various ships of the task group reported several unknown planes well outside the immediate radius of the formation, but that single bogey was reported again at 9:12, along with a friendly plane, bearing 310 degrees, about six miles out. There was nothing else within 25 miles of the formation. It was considered to be a very normal situation: everyone was used to the Japanese snoopers that ranged around the formation these days. Captain Buracker was quite pleased with the performance of his flight crews, and particularly the pilots and gunners—for he could boast about the 36 planes *Princeton*'s men had destroyed that morning, and that was a handsome number. One pilot was gone, but that was to be expected. War is a deadly and dangerous business and there are always casualties to offset the triumphs.

Admiral Sherman was nervous. He wanted to get that strike in the air. It had been scheduled for 9:00, and he was already late. He urged the captains of the carriers to get their planes out of the air, checked and refuelled and rearmed, and back to the mission at hand.

Captain Buracker was doing his best. He knew that some of his fighters would have various troubles when they came down. In fact, the first pilot to land had a damaged plane, and a bullet through his leg. Obviously he was not going on the mission to the Sibuyan Sea. But he kept after the air officer and the landing crews, and the fighters kept straggling in. It seemed forever today, getting them aboard, but they managed somehow. Around 9:35 the *Princeton* had landed ten of her fighters and still had two to go.

In operating, the formation moved into an area of low cloud cover, which meant the lookouts had to strain their eyes and still could not see very far from the ship.

Suddenly, at 9:38, one lookout shouted, "Bogey on the port bow."

Heads snapped. Sure enough, there it was.

At that moment the word came to the captain on the TBS (talk-between-ships-telephone).

"Dive bomber 160 in a dive." More heads snapped forward. But no one heard.

On deck the gasoline detail was busy filling up the fighters that had just landed, as the crew chiefs checked them over for battle damage and readiness.

No one heard the *Mobile*'s transmission because all attention was focused on the bomber and on the anti-aircraft guns of *Princeton* that were popping, snapping, and booming at the incoming Japanese plane.

Forward, the 20mm guns snapped, and the 40mm Oerlikons pumped.

"Hard left rudder," shouted the captain on the bridge, and the helmsman put it over 20 degrees to the left, maneuvering to avoid the attack.

In a moment the guns of *Princeton* were joined by the guns of other ships, and the air was filled with smoke and flying shells.

But then the Japanese zoomed down low, over the *Princeton* and dropped one 500-pound (250 kg) bomb.

It came whistling down. Then, Wham!

CHAPTER SEVEN

"No Immediate Concern"

The Japanese plane zoomed over the ship, and the gunners turned with it, as it moved. Guns from *Lexington* and the cruiser *Reno*, which were moving alongside the *Princeton*, also took the plane under fire as it pulled out of its dive at about 1,000 feet, levelled off right over *Princeton*, and flew aft. For a moment or two the plane could be seen, then the clouds grasped it and it disappeared. In a few minutes, the plane was found by the Combat Air Patrol of *Lexington*, and shot down into the sea.

On the bridge, Captain Buracker did not feel much concern. It was not unusual for a carrier to take a bomb. This one had hit about 15 feet off the centerline to port, about 75 feet forward of the after elevator. It would have been much worse, apparently, had it hit the elevator, for it might have knocked that vital mechanism out of working order, and that would definitely have put a crimp in operations. The hole was small, about 14 inches in diameter, and altogether it seemed to be the kind of problem that the damage control party could handle without overexertion. Captain Buracker visualized the control party putting a patch on the deck in a hurry and resuming operations.

When the bomb hit, the ship had changed course in its evasive action, but now the rudder was reversed and the *Princeton* returned to her formation course without having gotten too far from her assigned station. The captain sent a report to Admiral Sherman on the TBS:

"I have taken a bomb," he said. "Will keep you informed."

He went back to work then. There had hardly been any jarring on the bridge, and the ship was steaming along still comfortably at 24 knots. The navigator had automatically made a note of the position, which was 15 degrees, 21' North, 123 degrees, 31' East.

Admiral Sherman received the news without worry. His people had seen the Judy (dive bomber) come down on the *Princeton,* but they were not particularly worried either. It did not seem to the admiral that there was much danger to a big strong ship like the *Princeton* from one 500-pound bomb. He was discomfited of course because there had been damage, but considering the fact that more than 100 planes had been after the task group that morning, and only one plane had gotten through and delivered one small bomb, Admiral Sherman thought it was a fair morning's work.

But what the Admiral and Captain did not know was that the small bomb had been placed in precisely the position where it could do utmost damage to the *Princeton.*

Admiral Sherman was concerned enough, of course, that he asked Captain Buracker if he wanted to slow down. The captain said there was no reason to do so. There were fire hoses on deck, and the ship's working spaces were unimpaired.

But immediately after the bomb hit, thick black smoke was coming from the edges of the forward elevator. That was odd. The forward elevator was a long way from that bomb.

What had happened? The bomb had penetrated the main deck down to the second deck, set a fire in the scullery, which was amidships, on the third deck, immediately below the bomb hit. Also, a brilliant orange flame was observed in the bake shop, on the port side of the second deck.

Something untoward had certainly occurred.

One minute after the bomb hit, the situation seemed much more serious than before. The smoke was coming from the edges of the elevator, from the bomb hole in the flight deck, and from every access to the hangar deck aft of the carrier's island structure. The word was passed on the general announcing circuit and soon echoed through the ship.

"Fire in the hangar deck. Fire in the hangar deck."

Men began running

The Captain called Radar Plot, the Combat Information Center, which was the battle station of Commander J.W. Murphy, the tough, seasoned, stocky Executive Officer of the ship.

He was relieved—Murphy was not there—he had heard the general broadcast and was already on his way to the scene of the fire. He would be the captain's eyes and ears, for the captain's place was on his bridge, fighting for his ship.

Still, Captain Buracker was thinking in terms of continuing flight operations that morning.

He was distracted in that first minute by a report of a man overboard. Immediately the destroyer *Porterfield* was informed—it was the task group screen commander's ship— and the commander ordered the destroyer *Cassin Young* to make a rescue.

Cassin Young moved into the search pattern behind the *Princeton* and found the man—he had been blown overboard by the blast. The destroyer picked him up—and almost immediately her crew was sent to battle stations. Enemy planes were discovered at 23,000 yards. Thirteen miles may not seem very close, but at 200 miles an hour a diving plane can cover distance in a hurry. *Cassin Young* made ready to fight. There was a rain squall between the ship and the enemy planes, and she could not help but head into it. Low visibility, then, made it impossible to sight the planes until they had closed to about 9,500 yards. When they came in sight, fire was opened on them. They shot at a Betty that came close, and a fighter came in and took on the Betty too. The Betty began to flame. Who got him? The gunners or the plane? No one would ever know— but it was certain that the teamwork between the destroyer's gunners and the plane had not hurt anything. The Betty splashed into the sea, and the anti-aircraft fire ceased, for the air was filled with friendly planes.

Meanwhile, the situation aboard *Princeton* was changing rapidly.

Below decks, the bomb hit had been felt as a quick dull jar in Central Station, the chief damage control station of the ship. The First Lieutenant, Lt. Harry E. Stebbings, Jr., was in charge of damage control. But at this time he did not receive any immediate report from any station or from any repair party that a bomb had hit the ship, or that there had been any damage.

The mechanical devices this day were more effective than the humans. Almost immediately the fire alarm for the hangar began ringing. The First Lieutenant ordered the Conflagration Station to turn on the hangar sprinkling system. This station was located in the overhead of the hangar on the port side, amidships, very close to where the bomb hit. So there could be no mistake the order was repeated by a different officer, the damage control officer, speaking on a different circuit.

In the Conflagration Station, three men were stationed that morning, one of them manning the damage control circuit, one manning circuit to operations, and one as a standby and relief man. The men acknowledged the order from above, but almost immediately choking sounds could be heard on the communications system.

"I've been hit," said the talker.

Bomb fragments had shot through the walls of the Conflagration Station, wounding him. He stayed at his post, but he told the others how hot it was growing, so close to the fire.

In Central Station, the First Lieutenant wanted acknowledgment that the order to turn on the sprinkling system had been carried out.

But it was growing deadly in the Conflagration Station. It was so close to the center of the fire, and high in the air, that the cubicle was filled with smoke, and the men could not see. They were sweating in the heat, and the metal around them was heating up fast.

The two others in the room were driven out, but the talker stood fast.

"Request permission to abandon station," he gasped.

"Permission granted," came the word from Central Station, "but also the request that those sprinklers be turned on."

"Aye, aye, sir," said the talker, misunderstanding. "We are abandoning."

He did not make it.

The other two scrambled out, and then when the talker did not come with them, they tried to make it back inside to rescue him. But it was too hot. The smoke was black and dense and they could not see him, or find him, and they had to leave him, to save their own lives. They moved across the hot metal, and finally made their way outside the hangar into the blessed fresh air.

Everywhere, the men in the hangar were beginning to evacuate their action stations in the heat and smoke. But that was not the only reason. The bomb explosion had occurred in that line of six torpedo bombers which had been moved from the main deck down to the hangar to facilitate the recovery of the fighters before the armed planes were sent off on the morning strike against the Kurita fleet in the Sibuyan Sea.

All six of the TBM's had been fitted with full auxiliary wing tanks to help them on their long flight to come, and they carried their normal gasoline load as well. All were gassed up and all were loaded with torpedoes. The fire was burning, and the sprinklers had not come on.

In the aft end of the hangar a seaman reached the panel control box, fighting his way through the blackness and the smoke, and pushed buttons that would operate the hangar sprinklers. But the indicator lights did not come on, and nothing happened. Coughing, this man led out a two-and-a-half inch firehose from the connection at the port side. But something had happened to the water pressure, and not even a trickle emerged.

The hangar deck officer, Lt. (jg) Auclair, now got into the action. He ran to the fire station at the port side of the hangar, and turned on pressure on two hoses which were attached to a "Y" fitting. He then went amidships to try to turn on the hangar sprinkling system—and saw what was the matter, why the talker in the Conflagration Station had been unsuccessful. The control switches were smoking heavily from a short circuit. Something had happened to burn out the automatic system.

Just then the smoke became so black and thick at this station that the telephone talkers and everyone else were driven out of the area, overcome, or nearly so, by smoke. Some men had to be helped outside the hangar, into the cleaner air.

Lt. Auclair ran to the forward starboard catwalk, and there he wanted to get word to Central Damage Control station to turn the sprinkler valves on manually. It was the only way water could be brought into the deck.

All this happened in scarcely a minute. Indeed, here on the catwalk, Auclair encountered Commander Murphy, the Executive Officer, who had hurried to this vantage point from the Radar Plot Room and just arrived. In a moment Auclair had told the story: all the hangar deck people had been driven out by the fire, the talker in the Conflagration Station was dead at his post, and the other two had barely escaped with their lives.

Nor was that all of it.

As they talked, Executive Officer and hangar officer, a seaman ran up excited. The Conflagration Station had just blown out, he said. If there was any question about the talker, there was not now. He was definitely dead.

Anyone on the hangar deck now could remain there only

if wearing a gas mask. The flames were licking around one TBM in particular, the one closest to the bomb—and it was sending up the oil-black smoke that blinded the men. From the forward end of the hangar, men dragged hoses and began to spray down the plane and others.

From the shipfitter's room, aft of the fire, an attempt was made to haul hoses, but the men could get no pressure. On the upper deck, a damage control party began breaking out firehoses from forward to run them down to the hangar deck. Lt. (jg) Carson, the repair officer here, was in charge of the operation.

But the problem was to get that sprinkling system working and put out the fire before it got to the other planes—and the torpedoes.

Luckily, Commander Murphy's stateroom was not far from the catwalk where he was conferring with Lt. Auclair. When Auclair explained the difficulty, Murphy headed for his room, and picked up the ship's service telephone there to report that the sprinklers weren't working yet. What was needed, said the exec, was to get them turned on manually from the third deck. And it had to be done fast. Things were getting very rough in the hangar. It was virtually impossible to get anywhere near the fire.

Now First Lieutenant Stebbings moved quickly. He called Ensign Christie, one of his repair officers, and told him to get down to the log room on the third deck, on the starboard side of the ship, and see that the hangar deck valves were open. In a few moments Christie reported back. No, was the answer. Something had happened to the remote control mechanism—either it had been damaged by fire or by the explosion of the Japanese bomb—and the valves had not opened. He had opened them manually, and he had also gone nearby into the ship's barber shop and opened another valve, and now the water was passing through.

Another crisis: Repair Station V had just lost contact— that was the engineering repair station—and Christie must take some men and go down and find out what was happening there.

There was trouble in engineering.

In Main Engine Control, the bomb was felt as a heavy jar of the ship, but no one knew precisely what had happened. One flash of flame came down through the vent ducts and burned the chief of the watch. They knew there that something had happened, something serious. Lt. Comdr. Harry Long, the engineering officer, passed the word immediately over his engineering circuits to report damage. But no damage of any kind was reported just then. Still, one could not quite say that—no report at all was received from the After Fire Room. Commander Long picked up the telephone and tried to get the After Fire Room on one circuit, and then on another, and finally on the ship's service phone. No response. He did not know that in the After Fire Room, heavy black smoke had come in at once to fill the space. The blowers were slowed, the dampers closed, and that cut the smoke down a bit, but there was no communication with any other station.

In one short minute after the bomb hit, the Forward Engine Room was so full of smoke there was danger of suffocation for the men there. It was black with smoke, as dark as night. All hands were ordered to put on gas masks, and they did. But now more things began to happen. From above they could hear explosions (the gasoline tanks of the planes in the hangar deck) and smoke kept coming through the air vents even when they were closed tight. It began to grow hot, as well as smoky. The Forward Fire Room and the After Engine Room reported extreme heat—and when the word was passed that there was fire in the hangar deck, the men in the engineering spaces wondered if it was searching for them too.

Two minutes after the bomb struck, the gunners on the main deck, located aft and on the port side of the ship, reported that the heat was growing intense and smoke cut down their vision making breathing difficult. Stations on both sides of the ship, aft of the bomb, requested permission to abandon their stations.

That would be dangerous. Those gun stations were established for the protection of the ship. One Japanese plane had gotten through. It was possible that another might come in. If the after guns were abandoned, what might not happen in such circumstances? The gunnery officer, considering the request—denied it.

Stick it out for a while, he told the men; the ship needed them and so did their companions.

He was not unaware of the dangers, however, and he ordered the gunner's mates to watch magazine temperatures carefully in the ready service magazines which were located in spaces under the flight deck near the guns. If the temperature in any ready service magazine hit 100 degrees, the magazine was to be sprayed with water.

And now, the bomb site and the fire changed the whole nature of the ship. Men began to move back toward the fantail from amidships, for they could not pass the point where the bomb had fallen. Aft on the flight deck, Lt. Comdr. Curtis, the assistant air officer, moved off the landing signal platform where he had been stationed to bring the planes aboard. There obviously could be no more landings on the *Princeton* until the fire was brought under control and the hole in the deck was patched. He tried to work forward on the flight deck, but the heat and smoke stopped him. He and several of his men took shelter under the platform.

Three minutes after the bomb hit, Admiral Sherman called Captain Buracker on the TBS.

"How many planes do you have in the air?" he asked.

"Ten," was the reply.

Three minutes later, after a little time for reflection, Admiral Sherman was asking around among the other carriers. He learned that *Lexington* could take six of those planes on her flight deck, and he ordered the other four to come in on *Essex*.

So the planes found a new home for the moment, from

which they could rearm, regas, and stay in the operations against the Japanese fleet that was coming in from the west.

Seven minutes after the bomb struck, the First Lieutenant was frantically trying to determine the nature and extent of the fire and damage so he would know what must be done to bring the ship back under control. He learned that there was damage in the crew's galley and it was filled with heavy smoke. He was having trouble with the ship's communications system; he could not reach his Damage Control Stations. But he did learn that the men were alert, and that they were moving into the Chief Petty Officer quarters on the second deck aft, to break out firehoses and move forward with them against the fire in the hangar.

The men were moving. They found a fire in the after gasoline trunk, and put it out with CO2 bottles and fog nozzles. Next door there was another fire, and they broke out firehoses—but they had no pressure. A carpenter's mate went below to try to start the individual fire pumps in the area (which operated independently of the main system) but he did not have any power and so the pumps would not run. Somewhere in the system, the power had been knocked out by the fire and the short circuit. It was so bad in the area, that the telephone systems were out and the men fighting could not keep the First Lieutenant informed of their progress.

Chief Engineer Long called the bridge from the engine room and asked if there was any hope of controlling the fire.

Of course there was, said the Captain. Was there any question about it?

Things were bad down below, said the Chief, but they could keep on going if they had to. But the Captain ought to know one thing: he had lost all contact with the After Fire Room.

Perhaps they ought to slow down, said the Captain. Or even stop.

The Chief Engineer knew just how concerned the Cap-

The launching of *Princeton*, proud new carrier.

Princeton at sea—ready to fight.

Sometimes they used jeeps to jockey the planes around the flight deck.

It was a happy day when the ship's hoses were used to scour the flight deck.

Some of the men of Air Group 27, the *Princeton*'s team...

Commander Murphy (left), the exec, goes over a chart with a junior officer.

AOM 2c L.D. Aoevedo getting ready to load the guns of *Princeton*'s planes.

Princeton's plot room.

The air officer of the
Princeton (left), Lieutenant
Commander Harwood.

Lieutenant Moiteret (left),
navigator of the *Princeton*,
takes a sun shot, while
QM1C Honeycut gives him
a hand.

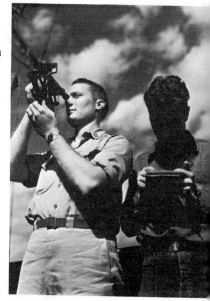

Captain Hoskins, on the bridge, ready for action...

The *Cassin Young* entering port.

The *Reno*.

Captain Buracker gives a press conference after one of *Princeton*'s many battles.

The *Birmingham* in better days.

The *Morrison* in camouflage.

The Japs came in, and one of them lobbed a little 500-pound bomb (250 kg) onto *Princeton*'s deck, in spite of this anti-aircraft barrage around her.

Princeton (left) badly hurt and in her own smoke, under air attack, with one of her rescuers alongside.

The trouble with steaming ahead to avoid further attack was that it fanned the fires.

All of the fleet could see that *Princeton* was in trouble.

From the decks of the little destroyers it was a long way up—too far, Captain Buracker discovered—for their hoses to be very effective.

One of the problems was that the *Princeton* overhung the other ships and the firefighters were in constant danger of being smashed between metal.

When *Birmingham* came alongside, the men snaked out the hoses; then some real progress in firefighting began.

Behind those men and that stream of water was the inferno of the hangar.

They kept bumping, and each bump meant disaster of some kind for one of the ships up against the carrier.

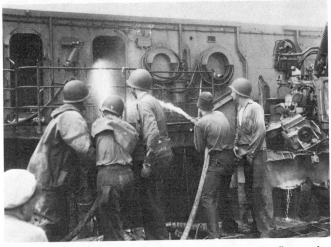

From here, *Birmingham*'s men could really get at the fire on the hangar deck.

Boats from the destroyers rescued hundreds of men that day.

An "overloaded ark" takes a line from its rescuers.

It seemed like confusion, but the men of the *Cassin Young* were performing heroically in the rescue.

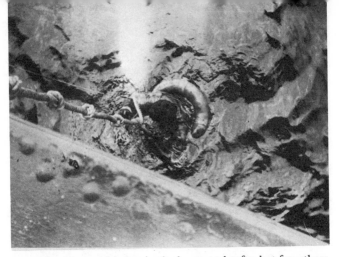

For some it was salvation in the boats and rafts, but for others there was no recourse but to swim for it. This seaman is safe enough, if uncomfortable, with life ring and lines and a knotted hawser to bring him in.

It was an explosion—not the Japanese bomb—that blew the elevator (right) akimbo.

Near the end...and just before the explosion that wracked the *Princeton* and smashed across the decks of *Birmingham*.

A group of survivors from the *Princeton* aboard the *Essex* after the battle to save the ship was fought and lost. Captain Buracker is in the middle of those kneeling, wearing the flight cap. Commander Murphy is to his left in the oversea cap.

A dramatic view of *Princeton*'s last stand.

tain must be to make such a suggestion. A warship simply did not stop on the high seas, unless it was absolutely essential. Particularly not in the middle of a battle, where a stopped carrier was a sitting duck for air attack and submarine attack. And they had no idea what was coming next. It was a measure of Captain Buracker's concern, and his courage that he would even suggest stopping.

But they were not to stop. No, said the Chief Engineer, it was not necessary as far as he was concerned at that moment.

He rang off, and called the First Lieutenant in the Central Damage Control Station. How about some more ventilation down below, he asked, for if they couldn't do something to help "the black gang" the boys would have to abandon the stations.

All right, said the First Lieutenant, he would try to do something for them by opening doors and hatches that gave onto the engineering spaces. Then he would try some exhaust ventilation.

In the After Engine Room, things were going badly at this point. A high pressure air line over the no. 3 main engine on the starboard side sprang a leak, and some men panicked and thought it was a main steam leak—which would have been very dangerous. In the darkness of the smoke it was hard to tell exactly what was leaking, and the men evacuated the After Engine Room, without securing the machinery, or reporting to main Engine Control, so the turbo generators in the After Fire Room began to slow down, unattended, and began to lose power needed on deck. The drop in voltage caused one of the fire pumps to stop, and that stopped the pressure to some of the mains aft. Men also evacuated their stations in the After Fire Room, but the lack of communication with the deck and the Central Damage Control Station prevented anyone from finding out that they had left this position.

Strange things began to happen. Steering aft shifted the alternate power supply. But stranger, by far, was the sounding of the fire alarms in these spaces where there was no fire. Something had gone awry with the fire system, and the sprinkling pump in the diesel generator room began running and its alarm screamed. In the darkness, the watch in the After Fire Room believed they had lost fire under no. 3 boiler, and they secured the equipment and evacuated. The propellers of the ship began to slow down.

Electrician mates were working with the alarm system and communications system, but could not get the circuits all restored. In Central Station the gasoline ventilation alarm bell was somehow triggered off, and then would not stop, which meant the First Lieutenant and his crew now had the clanging and noise of the alarm system to contend with as they tried to think and act. They knew only too well what might happen if this fire in the hangar deck continued to burn as hotly as it now was. The whole ship might go up in one big explosion.

At 9:48, ten minutes after the bomb hit, a good deal had been done to bring safety. For one thing, the gasoline mains forward had been drained, and the pipes filled with inert gas that would not explode if struck by a spark. Throughout the ship, men were coming up from below, driven up by smoke. Captain Buracker was growing worried.

By this time the ship was reverberating with small explosions. The gas tanks of the six bombers were going up, and of course, as each exploded, the black smoke increased, and so the fire spread. The captain could not understand why there was no pressure aft—it was some time before communications were restored and he got the picture. The Captain ordered the personnel out of the lower spaces, to come up on deck, because he did not want any men overcome with smoke and left to die below.

CHAPTER EIGHT

The Explosions

At 9:48 Admiral Sherman was on the TBS system, asking Captain Buracker how things were going. Under other circumstances the Admiral might have been impatient, for he was eager to get his air strike off the carriers and headed toward the Japanese before the day grew any older, and he now could see that whatever was wrong with *Princeton*, it was not going to be repaired by simply slapping a patch over the hole in the carrier's deck.

"Do you want to slow?" the Admiral asked Buracker.

This time Captain Buracker's reply was in the affirmative. Their speed of 24 knots was keeping the flames fanned and the fires going. If they were to cut back, perhaps it would be easier for the *Princeton* to put out the fire and get back into action before the afternoon was over.

Admiral Sherman knew how eager Admiral Mitscher and Halsey were for him to get his strikes under way. Still, without a question in a few moments came the order from the task group for the whole group to cut back to 18 knots. The men of *Princeton* complied gratefully.

The First Lieutenant was busily trying to correlate the activities of the damage control parties, with faulty communications. He learned, every few minutes, that the damage was worse than he thought and growing. The problem was the water supply, the inability to get water into the after lines which could play on the fire in the hangar and cut it back. The fire had spread upward and was playing on the flight deck, but here a damage control party was busy with hoses. That fire caused the Captain more concern than he might have felt otherwise, and he called down to Central Station for a report from the First Lieutenant. Actually, there was not enough information to give the Captain a report, and the First Lieutenant said so. He was still collecting information. He would report just as soon as he had it. It was hard to believe, but it was still only eleven minutes after the bomb struck the carrier.

Aft on the flight deck, the assistant air officer, Lt. Comdr. Curtis, went down in the After Ready Room with an idea. He picked up the phone and called Lt. Comdr. Harwood, the air officer, at air control. What if the ship could be turned out of the wind? Then the heat and smoke would be cut back, instead of carried aft the way it was. Right then, he said, he could see men being driven over the sides and off the fantail into the water.

The Captain got in touch with Admiral Sherman over the TBS radio.

"We are going 40 degrees to the right for better wind," he said.

The ship's course was changed to 105 degrees while the remainder of the task group remained on 065 degrees. *Princeton* began to move away from the safety of the group.

Admiral Sherman could not have a straggler—a sitting duck—left behind for the Japanese to hit at will. He detached the cruiser *Reno* and three destroyers to stay with *Princeton* and look after her. The *Reno* was singularly well-suited to the job, for she was an anti-aircraft cruiser of a new design, and she literally bristled with protective guns. Soon the word came that the destroyers *Gatling*, *Irwin*, and *Cassin Young* were to detach from the Force and join the stricken carrier, to add their anti-aircraft guns and to be prepared to work over any submarines that dared come within range. Those were the dangers, planes and submarines—the Japanese fleet units were still far too far away to bother the *Princeton*.

Princeton moved away, closely clearing the stern of the battleship *South Dakota*. Her troubles continued, too, for as she moved she lost her main TBS circuit—another short circuit caused by the fire, apparently. But such was the constitution of these new carriers that *Princeton* communications were not knocked out. There was a secondary TBS circuit, and when Admiral Sherman was notified of *Princeton*'s new problem, he ordered *Reno* and the other protective ships to guard that circuit for information from the carrier.

For some time now the small caliber ammunication and gasoline tanks had been exploding irregularly as they caught the intense heat. The ship's hangar deck was filled with heavy black smoke, and white smoke was emerging from all the seams of the flight deck. But the move to the right helped; there was no question about it. Immediately the smoke began to clear in the Main Engine Control Room.

Around 9:55 a new problem was presented. The hot water from the upper decks (fire-fighting water heated by the fires) was moving down into the Foreward Fire Room bilges and had almost reached the floor plates. Men in the fire rooms were suffering from the heat, and some were starting to pass out. The fire rooms asked for relief. The reports were made, but in the confusion they seem to have been ignored. No relief came to the Foreward Fire Room.

The fire was still making much smoke. Battle dressing stations below decks had to be abandoned, and Commander Sala, the chief medical officer, also ordered the four patients resident in the sick bay moved out, for their own comfort and safety. The main effort to help burned and hurt men took place in the wardroom, where some 20 men had now been give first aid treatment for burns. Other treatment was given in the After Battle Dressing Station in the CPO messing compartment on the second deck, but that would soon be abandoned due to the smoke and heat.

The planes kept burning—obviously all six of them

were afire by this time—and the little explosions kept recurring, felt as shocks in Central Station. The Engineering Repair Party came in to report six inches of water in the decks of the engineering spaces—and *hot* water. Also, Ensign Christie reported that there were 12 men trapped in the Executive Officer's office, on the port side, forward, and that they apparently were badly burned. Nobody could get to them because of the very hot water on the decks.

Water, steam, and fire were taking their toll. At 9:56 steering control was lost in the pilot house, and the steering emergency alarm began to blast through the air. Immediately steering aft took control (this was a well-organized ship). Captain Buracker stood on the bridge and gave his orders over a special circuit to the steersmen aft, who then executed them. Control of the ship was not lost for a minute. The Captain was worried, because of the fire and smoke streaming aft, lest the after steering compartment fill with smoke, but the quartermasters assured him that there was no smoke. They had begun to get some but had then shut the vent tight and no smoke was coming in.

Moving away at 18 knots, Captain Buracker was outside the vicinity of the task group in three or four minutes, and the *Reno* and the destroyers then began circling the carrier, to offer utmost protection against possible air attack

The crew on deck of the *Princeton* saw a new danger now. The white smoke creeping up under the flight deck seams meant bad news—spreading fire—and charring of the flight deck timbers. There would not be any more operations from the deck for a while; that much was certain. So the flight deck personnel were ordered to start jettisoning the planes on the deck, so they would not explode and become a menace to the men and the ship.

Over the fighters went, one, two, three, four, five. They splashed and floated for a moment, then went down—scores of thousands of dollars worth of equipment, but no men. Such was the war.

Then came 10:02.

The captain and others on the bridge were fairly well

satisfied with the way the fire was being fought. The gasoline detail of the ship had done a fine job, draining the tanks and filling the lines with inert gas that would not burn or explode. Thus, one of the grave dangers of a carrier fire was averted at the beginning of the trouble. The smoke was growing serious below, though, came the reports, and so the word was sent out:

''All hands topside.''

The men began to come up onto the main deck, from sick bay, from the forecastle, from the lower decks. Forward and aft men were abandoning ship, looking to the circling destroyers to pick them up. The wardroom battle dressing station was still open, however.

It came just then.

WHAMMMMMMMMMMMMMM!

An explosion the like of which no man on *Princeton* had seen or felt before. First a heavy blast vented upward through the flight deck and outward through the sides of the hangar, bulging and twisting the steel as though it was taffy. The entire flight deck was twisted, between the elevators, and the after elevator was removed from its pinnings and turned over on its back, as a cook turns a pancake.

A column of smoke rushed upward, and soon reached a point a thousand feet in the air, visible for miles around. It was black and gray with white underpinnings.

The first explosion blew men overboard from the gun mounts on the edges of the decks, men from the 40mm guns and the 20mm guns. No one knew at the moment how many men were lost, but two 40mm guns on the port side after were completely destroyed, and so were five 20mm guns. Nor were the blown the only casualties, many men were burned and hurt by flying shrapnel from their own guns, and three men were reported hanging from the radio antenna booms which extended out from the port quarter.

The tempo of action increased. Captain Buracker ordered a destroyer to close on the ship and pick up the men in the water. *Cassin Young* was designated.

The gunnery officer had lost all contact with the guns on the fantail and reported that these stations were isolated from the rest of the ship. Then, frantically, he called the First Lieutenant at the Damage Control Central Station, to discover the condition of head and smoke below decks. How were the magazines? That is what he wanted to know in particular. Lt. Moreland, the assistant damage control officer, assured him that at the moment everything was all right. But "Guns" was less than satisfied—for at that moment the circuit went dead. It was anything but comforting for a man worried about the ship blowing sky high.

Then came the second explosion. It was 10:03. It was slightly forward of the first—probably another torpedo on one of the planes. Gray white smoke again rose high in the air, not as high as the first time, and flames shot up over the ship. The flight deck buckled completely and gave off a blast of heat coming from the hangar below.

Two minutes went by. "Guns" asked Captain Buracker to move all the men at the after gun stations forward to escape the smoke and heat. The gunner's mates were told to sprinkle down all their ready service magazines, and to jettison all ready service ammunition on the gun shields before leaving their posts.

10:05—the ship was rippled and jarred by the most severe explosion yet felt. Gray smoke again, and a plume of white, back up to 1,000 feet above the *Princeton*. This time part of the flight deck actually blew up, the hangar bulged out and ripped, and the forward elevator blew up.

A minute later—another explosion. The smoke was gray and oily black, and followed by intense flame from below decks.

These three explosions drove new blasts of smoke into the forward engine room spaces. The telephone talkers began to cough and choke, and had to abandon their telephones. The chief engineer called the bridge, and asked the Captain how bad it was. The Captain was noncommittal. He instructed the chief to get the people on deck if things were impossible down there, but to secure before he left.

The First Lieutenant gave up on the after hose system, and ordered Ensign Christie to close the valves that led there, so as to preserve the ship's fire control system for use against the forward part of the ship. He was sure the explosions had twisted and wrecked the whole system in that area anyhow, and to leave things alone would impair the ship's firefighting efficiency. He was worried anyhow, because the lights were flickering—a very bad sign as far as the power system was concerned.

Admiral Sherman learned of the explosions—he could scarcely help seeing them himself, and ordered the cruiser *Birmingham* to stand by. No one could tell what might happen now.

These explosions had blown at least 15 men overboard and injured another dozen or more. The assistant air officer, Lt. Comdr. Curtis, ordered the men who crowded to the fantail to begin climbing down the lines over the side. They would have to get off the ship. Things were growing too rough aft, and there was no way of getting forward on any deck. Too much heat, fire, and smoke.

The destroyers saw, and moved in as close as they dared. The men clustered around the life rafts, but the rafts here marked with red, which meant they were to be saved aboard for the Ship's Rescue Party, the last group of men who would go overboard. Discipline did not break down. The red-painted rafts were left. The men cut loose the floater nets and began going down the lines to reach them. Others jumped into the water instead. But there was no panic, no apparent fright. The men swam and clung to the floater nets and waited for the destroyers.

With that 10:05 explosion, looking down from the bridge, Captain Buracker could see an open fire in the hangar, visible through the pit of the forward elevator, which was now tilted on one end of the elevator well. Smoky orange flames swept into the elevator pit. A four-by-four timber was thrown high into the air and struck a lookout, seriously injuring him and felling him. (He was transferred to a destroyer but died later that day). He was the only one hurt on the bridge, although a piece of supporting girder about 14 feet long was flung up over the open bridge and struck the flight deck crane arm—then stuck there.

All communications went out then, except the Captain's command circuit and he ordered the men up top. *Princeton* was really in trouble, for the first time. She had no communication with other ships, conditions on the bridge were growing terrible. Bridge and island personnel were directed to the flight deck forward, and they started down the forward side of the splinter shield and over the pedestal of the flight deck crane. There was a vertical ladder that ran up the inboard side of the island structure, but it was too hot, and the smoke prevented anyone from using it.

Down below, the Central Station was shaken violently by these last explosions, and the General Alarm began to sound. The First Lieutenant told an electrician's mate to cut the wires, and stop it and he did, but not before it had begun to ring—and that ringing told some men on the ship that it was a signal to abandon ship. That was not the signal for abandoning ship, but the men were looking for some action and they believed this was an emergency signal because communications had gone out. Some men began to abandon.

There was a call from the bridge and Lt. Moreland tried to answer it, but just as he picked up the phone the system went out. And then another explosion was felt, muffled, but definite.

In the engine room it was equally bad. Conditions, by the officers' definition, had become untenable even before the 10:05 explosion. This brought a flash through the vent lines, and electrical flashes, meaning danger. Steam was falling in the boilers aft, and amidships. The fire control system seemed to be losing its pressure. The chief engineer tried to call the bridge. No answer. No phone service. He considered the Captain's last order, and passed the word.

"All engineering personnel secure machinery and go topside."

What this meant, of course, was that the ship had lost its power and was about to go dead in the water. When the order was heard in the steering compartment aft, the men there asked the Captain if he wanted them to abandon their posts too. He said not yet—that they should remain for the time being. The communication was lost—the phones went out—and finally the steering compartment was reached by the bridge on the ship's service telephone, on an emergency system, and the men were told to get up on deck.

The Captain also called the men at Central Station to tell them to come up on deck, but there was no answer. They had already started, for no one knew when there would be another explosion that might blow the ship entirely out of the water. The fires were licking around compartments where bombs and torpedoes were stored, and everyone knew that anything could happen.

In the wardroom the lights went out. The smoke and fumes grew so strong that it was necessary to take the wounded to the forecastle.

Commander Murphy had led a party of repair specialists in fighting the fire from the forward part of the ship. But now these explosions drove him and his people off the catwalk, the metal grew hot and they had to hurry away. He and Lt. (jg) Carson, the Repair 1 officer, went to the flight deck, and joined the navigator who was directing several hose parties in fighting the fire, now that they could reach it through the forward elevator opening.

Things were growing very bad in the forward air defense area up by the island, and the navigator took one hose and tried to play it up there, to help the people escape. Just then the water pressure dropped. So the navigator dropped the hose. It was a good try, but the pressure would not reach so far.

Chief Engineer Long and Lt. Stasney, the officer of the watch, were the last men out of the engine room, and they made sure all the enlisted men were out before they left. They went up the starboard hatch to the third deck, and then up forward, and to the second deck, where they followed behind the men emerging from Central Station, and the radio room. The third deck was smoky and hot, but it was a relief to get up out of the engineering, where the heat was nearly unbearable. Altogether, some 100 men moved as quickly as they could from these deep spaces toward the light and sunshine. The Chief Engineer stopped them and made sure there was an orderly retreat. Half the men were sent to the main deck and through the wardroom and out to the forecastle. The others went forward on third deck and then up the forward ladders. He wanted to avoid panic, and in darkness (for only emergency lighting was on) the men might grow frightened.

The men did not panic. Not even when they reached the forecastle and the word was passed that the ship was about to take another air attack. They were ordered to take cover inside the ship. But then the all clear was passed, and the men went back to the forecastle.

Now, men on the fantail were leaving the ship as fast as they could scramble down into the water. Ensign O'Connor, the fourth division officer, and Lieutenant Bradley, the assistant first lieutenant, made sure that all the injured men and all they could find aft left the fantail. Some 300 men, trapped in the after part of the ship, made their way to the fantail and scrambled into the water—including most of the engineering people and the after repair party. Then the two officers followed. No panic here either.

It was comforting for the men in the water to see the friendly bulk of the destroyer *Irwin* moving close in to them. Commander D.B. Miller was standing in close, astern the carrier, and then moved alongside the port side to pick up personnel and help fight the fire with her hoses. The men of *Irwin* were conscious of a steady stream of small explosions, apparently coming from forty millimeter ammunition down below. The Captain ordered men stationed by all the magazine flood cocks on the destroyer, and removed exposed ammunition from the starboard side of the ship, lest *Irwin,* too, get in trouble from this heat.

He looked up at the fire. It seemed to be concentrated

amidships, just aft of the elevator. He moved in close to the carrier, but the high seas now took over, and smashed the destroyer into the port side of the carrier forward, so he backed on all engines to keep from damaging his ship, and cleared the ship astern. Now he could see men abandoning the *Princeton* at all points clear of the fire. (This came after the misunderstanding about the ''Abandon Ship'' order.)

Forward of the bridge, Captain Miller could see, the carrier was undamaged. Eight planes stood on the flight deck, still intact, armed, and fuelled, ready for action.

CHAPTER NINE

To Save a Ship

Captain Buracker was not sure he could save the ship, but he was certainly going to try. He had seen the smoke and raging fire in the hangar, and he had felt the breath of flame that forced him to move the men off the island. He directed them to abandon, and then went forward himself, to confer with Commander Murphy. They would now go into Salvage Control, Phase One, he said. That meant all the people not needed to fight the fire would leave the ship.

Admiral Sherman aboard the *Essex* was concerned when the explosions came, and he not only ordered *Birmingham* to stand alongside the carrier, but the destroyer *Morrison* as well. Sherman would try to maneuver in the area so as to stay as close to *Princeton* as possible, but he knew that to conduct flight operations he would have to move around with the wind, and that he would be 50 or 60 miles away from time to time.

At 1030 the *Irwin* again maneuvered alongside the *Princeton*, about 30 feet away, and then moved in close and secured on her port bow, with the overhang of the carrier projecting over the destroyer. All the projecting masts and booms broke off in the rubbing process, but that was to be expected under the circumstances.

Seven minutes after she came alongside there was another explosion on *Princeton*, which threw burning debris onto the destroyer. It came from the after end of the hangar, and was accompanied by shrapnel—which again meant the ammunition was burning and exploding.

Princeton was in serious trouble about fighting the fire. She had no water pressure, and she needed aero foam. *Irwin* directed her hoses on the flames, but she was so much lower than the carrier that her fire fighters had trouble getting their spray directed at the flames. At least, however, the damage control parties and other men of *Princeton* were able to make their way onto the decks of *Irwin* and escape. The damage control men then made it around the bridge of the destroyer, and moved to the hangar deck of the carrier to fight the fire with *Irwin*'s hoses. The best place on the destroyer—the only effective position—for operation of a hose was the searchlight stand. And while all this was going on, the destroyer's rescue crews kept bringing men aboard from *Princeton*'s bow.

All but 490 men would now abandon ship, and those 490 would fight the fire.

The *Princeton* was now dead in the water, which decreased the draft on the fire, but also left her wallowing in the heavy swell. Lt. Carson, the Repair 1 officer, went aboard *Irwin* to advise the Captain of *Princeton*'s state and to see if he could get some foam and better direction of the hoses from the destroyer.

On the carrier, men were climbing down the knotted ropes on the ship's bow, and some jumped directly into the water from the forecastle, which was a dangerous procedure, for it was a long way down. The First Lieutenant ordered them to belay that—and the men did. They were behaving very well, obeying orders quickly and readily. The next order from the First Lieutenant was to throw the 40mm empty cases of ammunition on the forecastle over the starboard side for rescue purposes. He also told the ship's boatswain to make ready for a tow. The boatswain had already rigged the port anchor chain for towing, and the First Lieutenant checked the work, then went forward to the foreward elevator pit to help fight the fire.

Elsewhere on the ship men were throwing life rafts into the water, and other men were getting into the water and boarding them.

The trouble, as Captain Buracker could see, was that when the ship lost power, the firefighting potential of the carrier was lost too. *Irwin* was working gallantly—taking on about 700 of the ship's personnel, playing hoses on the fire, and pulling men out of the water, but she could not do the job. She was too small, too low in the water.

The next phase called for cutting down to 240 men to remain on the ship, but the failures in internal communications made it impossible to carry out such an orderly program. The problem was that many of the men had misunderstood orders and abandoned ship, believing they were told to do so. So while Commander Murphy had men aboard the carrier to fight the fires, they were not the organized crew he expected to use. What he had expected to keep were salvage party and engineering personnel. But most engineering people had either left the stern or had gone to the bow and been taken off by *Irwin*. So Murphy sent word to the forecastle to stop any more men from leaving the ship. The orders were obeyed with readiness: there was no malingering, it was only a question of misunderstandings.

An air raid was now beginning. On their radar screens, the destroyers and cruisers around *Princeton* caught glimpses of numerous bogies, and they rallied around the dead ship to be sure they could cover her, because as she sat there, motionless, she was virtually "a sitting duck."

The anti-aircraft cruiser *Reno* circled the carrier in close, clockwise. One enemy plane came nosing in, and she shot it down with her main battery. A minute later she found another plane close in and shot that one down too. No others came close enough to endanger the stricken carrier.

The action was continuous among the rescue ships now, and it is shown in the message log of Destroyer *Irwin* for this time. (Hatchett is *Princeton*. The other names refer to the *Morrison, Irwin*, and *Gatling* alongside. The orders are from the senior officer. *Bayonet* is *Birmingham*.)

1000 Go along port side of Hatchett for fire and rescue work
1002 Close Hatchett
1030 From this side can't tell whether fire is coming under control or not
1031 Roger
1033 All stand by to pick up survivors from Hatchett
1040 If you can get another DD alongside can control fire in Hatchett
1040 Small boys [destroyers] do the rescuing and Bayonet screen
1048 Assist Hatchett in fire fighting as you can
1050 Desire Bayonet to come alongside and pump water. Reliance remain alongside and other rescue survivors
1051 Hatchett requests you come closer along side
1116 Reliance coordinate with rescue work.

During this time *Irwin* cast off for the swells were throwing her farther under the overhang of *Princeton*. She lost her starboard torpedo director and 40mm director, her pelorus, starboard anchor, and one section of the overhang caved in the starboard side of her bridge. The banging was also wrecking her bridge superstructure and the forward five-inch guns. She had to virtually abandon her own bridge and take steering aft to be sure no men got hurt by the contact between ships, and she suffered a number of short circuits and electrical fires herself. Soon it became apparent to *Irwin*'s skipper that he was doing very little but destroying United States property. In the position they occupied, they could scarcely put out the fires, they could hardly stream water at them.

The Captain ordered *Irwin* to pull away, and to concentrate on picking up the men in the water. He had noticed in recent minutes, too, that the swell was increasing in the wind, and this made it even harder to fight the fire—while the wind made the fires increase in intensity.

When the water pressure aboard *Princeton* failed at about ten minutes past ten, there was very little the men could do to fight the fire that threatened their ship and lives. They did get the gasoline handy-billy, a portable pump, from the repair locker on the forward deck center, and started it running. It was their major weapon now. The gunnery officer sent men into the officers' area to pick up additional 1.5-inch hose where it was stowed. But this was much like trying to put out a forest fire with a garden hose, and everyone knew it.

What had to be done was get at least one big ship alongside, with many hoses and a good deck height, relative to the *Princeton*. It was not easy to make this request known, for the electrical communications network of the carrier was stone dead, and trying to use semaphore flags and portable blinker was very unsatisfactory because of smoke, haze, and rain in the squalls that passed over the ships. But the message was received by *Birmingham* that she was needed to fight the fire, and she came up at 1055 and put her starboard bow alongside *Princeton*'s port bow, just as *Irwin* moved away, still shocked by the damage she had taken. Lines were run from the *Birmingham* to the forecastle of the carrier.

Captain Thomas B. Inglis, the commander of the *Birmingham*, had been giving a good deal of thought to the problem of fighting the fire aboard the carrier, with the resources at hand. Luckily for all, he was an experienced officer, with plenty of time at sea.

Captain Inglis was a Michigander, born in 1897 at Houghton Lake, where he grew up and went to school until appointed to the Naval Academy in 1914. His first sea service was on the USS *Kearsarge*, a coast battleship which operated with the Atlantic Fleet in World War I. He served then on several battleships until 1921, when he went to destroyers in the Pacific fleet. Then there was a period of study—he attended the navy's postgraduate school at Annapolis and received a Master of Science degree from Harvard University. He went back to battleships as a communications specialist, and served on the *West Virginia* and the *California*.

Communications continued to be his specialty in the 1930's until he secured command of the USS *Hatfield*. Later he was navigator of the cruiser *Houston*. For a time he was commander of a naval cargo vessel, the USS *Algorab*, but in 1942 he became Deputy Director of naval Communications, and served in Washington until August, 1943, when he took command of the *Birmingham*.

First operations for the cruiser under him were with the fast carriers, attacking Tarawa, Wake, and Peal islands, and supporting the landings in the Solomons and the Philippines. Captain Inglis received the Bronze Star for his operations at Saipan in the summer of 1944, and the Silver Star for his work in covering the withdrawal of the *Canberra* and the *Houston* when they were torpedoed in the battle of Formosa.

For a long time before today, he had been thinking of the problems of saving a carrier on fire, because he could see that in air operations this was a constant threat. He had long ago decided that if it was left to him, he would take his ship alongside the windward side of the carrier, close aboard, put his hoses over and fight the fires from the carrier's decks, driving them downwind until they were extinguished.

Now, with the new order from Admiral Sherman, Captain Inglis moved in as the senior officer present of the group around *Princeton*—which meant that he was in charge of the firefighting and salvage operations.

He instructed the destroyers to lay off whatever else they were doing and concentrate on recovering the *Princeton*'s people in the water. When he made that decision there were probably a thousand men in the water, men coming off the ship under the mistaken belief they had been ordered to abandon. There were probably 50 men, plus the Captain and his chief aides, on the deck of the carrier.

So the destroyers were called to action, and *Reno* with her excellent sound gear and bristling with anti-aircraft guns, was told to cover the little fleet against air attack and submarine attack. He had his own big ship, the *Birmingham*, the *Reno,* and the four destroyers, *Morrison, Irwin, Gatling,* and *Cassin Young* with which to work.

He warped *Birmingham* in alongside, and virtually pushed two of the destroyers away, because in their zeal the captains did not respond immediately to his instructions.

Essex announced that she was sending a division of fighters to work as Combat Air Patrol above the little fleet, and they were soon in the air above. They could stay aloft until 1:15 that afternoon, the leader told *Birmingham.* Then it was "pancaking time," meaning they would either land on their carrier or somewhere else—perhaps even in the water.

Reno was also ready, so the air patrol was as complete as it could be. Just before Inglis had taken charge, there had been a little confusion because of the communications failure on *Princeton. Birmingham* asked *Reno* to continue circling the group, while *Irwin* announced that *Princeton* wanted *Reno* to come and pump water on her port quarter. Inglis announced that *Birmingham* was coming alongside the stricken carrier, and told *Irwin* to remain for the moment, for *Cassin Young* to drop back and assist *Morrison* and *Gatling* in picking up those survivors. *Reno* would assist in pickup on the next time she came around on her circle.

But, not knowing that Captain Inglis had a plan for action, Captain Buracker was doing the best he could, frantically asking *Reno* for help.

1056 *Reno* from *Irwin*: *Princeton* requests you come alongside starboard with water.

Irwin from *Reno*: *Birmingham* in charge. *Birmingham* coming alongside now.

Reno from *Birmingham*: Comply with *Princeton*'s request.

Aboard destroyer *Gatling* the crew was jubilant, for they claimed part of the credit for shooting down the two planes that had attacked a few minutes earlier. But they complied with the orders. They put the ship's whaleboats over the side, rigged netting for climbing, and began to pick up men in the water.

Morrison was doing the same.

As for *Birmingham*, she nudged up against *Princeton* and her crew was ready for action. While they had been coming along, Captain Inglis had ordered the crew to lead out all the fire hoses on the ship, put full pressure on the fire mains, and make every preparation for fighting those *Princeton* fires the moment they arrived. Captain Inglis was confident that he had the best ship possible for the job at hand, with superior equipment, great deck space for working the hoses, and a very fine pumping capacity and hose capacity.

Birmingham came alongside *Princeton*, and her men were ready to begin fighting the fires.

It was just about 11 o'clock in the morning, not quite an hour-and-a-half since that single Japanese bomber had dropped his lucky bomb.

With the coming of *Birmingham* to help, hopes rose again, for it was almost as if *Princeton* had her power back and could fight the fires herself.

CHAPTER TEN

The Avengers

At 11 o'clock, when *Birmingham* brought her port bow up against the burning carrier, Admiral Sherman and the task group were moving away, not to desert the stricken ship and her sisters, but to launch planes and get on with the work at hand, the destruction of the Japanese fleet that had set out to defend the Philippines from invasion.

So planes from *Princeton*'s task group were moving out to avenge the bomb.

The Japanese had been found—some 26 ships—in the Sibuyan Sea, just off the southeast tip of Mindoro Island, on a course of 015 degrees. The Japanese force was reported to be divided into two groups. The western group of ships was assigned to the pilots of *Essex*, by Commander T.H. Winters of *Lexington*, the strike leader. *Langley* and *Lexington* planes were assigned to the eastern group of ships, and the planes from *Princeton*, which had landed elsewhere, were assigned to the mission of the ship they had joined.

Here is the story of *Essex*'s planes that day, in their search for revenge against the Japanese.

Eight fighters led by Lt. Comdr. J.F. Rigg, took off on a strike mission against the Task Force, and escorted bombers and torpedo bombers to and from the target area. They joined the planes of *Lexington* and *Langley* in the air and divided into two groups. The groups became separated in a long front some 50 miles from the carriers, but later they rejoined, and then began searching for the enemy fleet. It was found by Lt. (jg) C.B. Milton—and when he reported, a division of fighters dove down from 13,000 feet, dropping their bombs at 3,000, and then strafing. The idea was to cut down the anti-aircraft fire. The fighters came in, dropped their bombs, and then came back to strafe, covering the heavier planes as they made their runs.

Commander James Mini led the dive bombers, which joined up with planes of *Lexington* and *Langley,* and, because his flight instruments were out, he led them over the front instead of through it. Thus he found the Japanese before the others did. Lt. John David Bridgers was the first to see the enemy—he spotted a ship off Banton Island and gave the signal. A fighter moved down and confirmed.

The planes of *Essex* orbited for 15 minutes, above Dumali Point, Mindoro, waiting for the planes from *Lexington.* Then they began to attack the two groups, *Lexington* taking the eastern force and *Essex* planes taking the western ships.

Commander Mini led his five-plane division through a hole in the clouds, from 13,000 feet through 6,500 feet, and he dived on the *Nagato* class battleship he saw there, making three hits and a hit on an *Atago* class cruiser that was next to the battleship. Lieutenant Bridgers went farther and attacked a battleship he believed to be the *Musashi,* one of Japan's largest and finest, and saw three hits.

In retiring, Commander Mini's plane was hit in the gauntlet of anti-craft fire they had to run, from the Japanese cruiser and destroyer screen. An anti-aircraft shell hit the empennage of the plane, damaged his elevator controls, his magnetic compass, and wrecked his tail hook. His wing man, Lt. (jg) L.E. Nelson escorted him back to the American fleet, and he made a water landing near a destroyer. He could not come down on a carrier, with his damaged plane.

The torpedo bombers had a more difficult time. They

launched just before eleven o'clock, and then flew toward the target. But they hit bad weather, many squalls, and roamed around until they found a major force, ten miles north of Romblon Island, sighting it first through heavy cloud cover, and spotting the wakes of the ships as they moved.

Below them they sighted two battleships, a force of five cruisers and five destroyers. The torpedo bombers were divided into two eight plane divisions, with Lt. C.H. Sorensen leading one and Lt. Comdr. Lambert the other.

Lt. Sorensen and Lt. L.G. Muskin were the first to drop. They attacked two of the battleships, which were nearly in column. Lt. Muskin went in to 700 feet at 250 knots, and 1,300 yards out he dropped his torpedo. He said he had an ideal shot, but he could not see the result because the anti-aircraft fire was so intense. Others said he scored a hit amidships on the second battleship.

Lt. Sorensen attacked the other battleship, which he identified as the *Musashi*. His torpedo hit directly aft on the starboard side, and exploded.

Below, the battleships began a long turn to starboard to avoid the planes, and this meant the other pilots had to attack on the turn, which made life more difficult. But on the other hand, at one point the two battleships were nearly bow to stern, which made a good target.

Lt. Comdr. Lambert attacked the *Musashi*, and thought he scored a hit. So did Ensign A.R. Hodges. Then in came Lt. (jg) R.L. Bentz, Lt. (jg) S.M. Hollady, and Lt. (jg) H.A. Goodwin, all dropping on the *Musashi*. Two explosions were definitely seen, and a third was suspected; two were forward of the bridge and aft of the stack.

Lt. (jg) Hollady dropped from 1,000 feet at 290 knots, to a range of 1,600 yards, and his crew said they were sure of another explosion. Lt. Goodwin was sure he got a hit. One would expect, perhaps, that so many hits would have blown the Japanese battleship out of the water, but this was the *Musashi*, and she had the thickest armor plate in the world. She carried 19-inch guns, and she was supposed to be "unsinkable." Yet when last seen by the pilots of Sherman's task group that day, she was down at the bow and streaming oil. The Japanese were learning that there was no "unsinkable" ship.

Three other pilots now attacked the second battleship, which turned out to be the *Kongo*, an older ship but still a very powerful weapon. Lts. R.D. Chaffe, and J.C. Crumley all came in on this ship, and were very optimistic about their results. Meanwhile Lt. W.S. Burns and Lt. (jg) O.R. Bleech dropped on a cruiser that was moving fast, until she was hit, then lost speed and dropped out of the formation. In this attack Lt. Bleech was hit, and did not see what happened next. But Lambert said he saw that the torpedoes ran true and exploded against the ships.

Lt. (jg) M.P. Deputy dropped on a cruiser. Lt. (jg) E.F. Lightner dropped on a cruiser too. Others said both had hits. In fact, only two erratic torpedoes were reported by the whole force and the pilots felt sure they had done some major damage to the Japanese fleet.

Two pilots, Lts. (jg) Paul B. Southard and W.F. Axtman failed to come back after the attack, and one of these was seen to go down in flames. The other made a hard water landing, just outside the destroyer screen of the Japanese and his fate was not known then. (Later it was learned that Lt. Axtman was saved, along with one of his crewmen.)

The Japanese had fought hard, using some techniques not familiar to the Americans, including using heavy guns to throw up water spouts in front of approaching torpedo planes. But it was noted that the Japanese did very little maneuvering. That seemed odd to the pilots.

Altogether they came home satisfied with their mission. Meanwhile, Admiral Sherman, crippled as he was by the inability to use full plane force of *Princeton*, was still carrying the battle against the Japanese.

It was a busy time. Hardly had the strike above been launched against the Japanese fleet in the Sibuyan Sea than Admiral Sherman learned from returning search planes of many targets in the Manila area where they had been sent in the morning, including several cruisers and destroyers. But the Sibuyan Sea force was considered the first target, because they were obviously heading toward San Bernardino Strait, and that would mean trouble for Admiral Kinkaid's Seventh Fleet unless they were turned back.

There were still too many Japanese snoopers about for comfort. One thing about the Japanese system—their almost constant presence tended to keep the Americans alert. They never knew whether the bogies on the screens were flying boats conducting routine missions, or bombers coming in laden with torpedoes.

Now Admiral Sherman began to suspect that there was more in the air and in the water than met the eye. Many of the planes that had come in to attack that morning had been carrier types, and he believed that there was an enemy carrier force somewhere off to the northeast, which must be dealt a blow before it could smash the Third Fleet. At 1155 he launched a search consisting of two fighters and a bomber in each of several sectors to the northeast—or he was preparing to do so when things began to happen. Sherman was also preparing to launch a second strike of bombers and torpedo planes against the Japanese in the Sibuyan Sea. The strike did get off, but just then there came word of another Japanese force of planes coming in, and lest *Lexington, Essex,* or *Langley* meet the fate of *Princeton,* Admiral Sherman got his fighters in to the air to intercept the Japanese and knock them down.

In came the enemy from the northeast, and the flight was broken up before it could reach a point much closer than 50 miles from the formation. While the fighting was still in progress, another group was reported, 90 miles out and to the east. All available fighters from the three carriers were scrambled, and the raid was again intercepted, this time 25 miles out. Some Japanese planes did filter through. None found the helpless *Princeton* with her escorts, but six or eight dive bombers came in on *Lexington* and *Essex*—and three of them were shot down in flames. The others escaped or went quietly into the sea.

The second strike hit the Japanese, who were really feeling the punches in the Sibuyan Sea. In all, 259 flights were made from American carriers against the Japanese in that sea that day, and it was small wonder that some Japanese felt that everywhere they turned there was another American plane. That day, for example, *Musashi* took 19 torpedoes before she sank. Three other battleships, *Yamato*, *Nagato*, and *Haruna* were all damaged; no one could say precisely by whom. It was a known fact that the American pilots were always optimistic and upbeat about the hits they scored on the Japanese, but the results of this day certainly bore out the fact that they were fighting hard. Heavy cruiser *Myoko* was damaged that day, so badly she had to return to Japanese water and could not fight on. The Japanese were thrown into confusion, and Admiral Kurita lost several valuable hours, because he had a timetable to meet and if it was not met the attack he planned could hardly hope to succeed.

But having used all his fighters to stave off attack, Sherman had none left to accompany the bomber search planes out to the northeast. Thus can be shown the interdependence of the carrier group. The damage to *Princeton* slowed affairs considerably. Sherman did sent out some search planes without fighters, and they did find an enemy task force to the east, but by this time it was too late to launch a strike. Had *Princeton* not been hit that morning, and had she been able to participate in the battle as she had before, then affairs might have been quite different, and the northern force of Admiral Ozawa, which did not get into the action at all on October 24, might have been struck that day, and Admiral Halsey might have remained where he was, or left some of his force to guard San Bernardino Strait and protect the Seventh Fleet from the Kurita force.

But *Princeton* was not only hit, she was in dire trouble.

CHAPTER ELEVEN

Progress Report

On the *Birmingham*, Captain Ingles fought the fire on *Princeton*. The two ships had to be held together with lines, because the carrier with its high sides made faster leeway than the cruiser. This was ticklish—the hoses kept breaking and carrying away—and the *Birmingham* had to maneuver with her engines to keep the ships together. The Inglis plan was to move from front to back, fighting and putting out the fires in the bow, and moving aft, gradually moving the *Birmingham* in relation to the *Princeton*.

The men of *Princeton* were still trying to help their ship too. A semaphore message was sent to *Irwin* to move around to the stern and try to play a hose. *Irwin* was instructed to other duty but relayed the message to *Cassin Young*. And aboard *Princeton*, Commander Sala, the senior medical officer, and Lt. Oesterle, a dental officer, worked with three pharmacist mates to take care of any casualties who needed help. Meanwhile, they spent their efforts at manning hoses to put the fires out.

After about half an hour Captain Inglis called for a volunteer fire party to go aboard *Princeton*. Lieutenant Alan Reed, the assistant first lieutenant of *Birmingham*, then led a party of 38 volunteers on to the burning carrier. Their job was certainly dangerous: the fire forward had been put out, but in the after elevator pit, 50 calibre machine gun bullets were popping like popcorn and the fire was burning in the torpedo workshop—which certainly did not augur well for the future. This was particularly true because the ship had taken on a supply of napalm for ground operations and since there was no ready place to stow it, the napalm had been housed in the torpedo workshop, aft of the hangar on the starboard side. This napalm had apparently caught fire and was burning.

At about 11:30, the fires forward kept flaring up, so the gasoline handy-billy was brought forward and used to extinguish each little blaze as it flared forth. This freed the big hoses of *Birmingham* for more important work. But in about 45 minutes the handy-billy ran out of fuel, and the men had to scurry about. All they could find—or reach—was aviation gas, and it was too powerful for the handy-billy. The pump would run for four or five minutes, heat up and cut out, and then the process would have to be started once again.

Men from *Birmingham* and *Princeton* were cooperating beautifully. The air office, the First Lieutenant, and Chief Shipfitter White took a party of enlisted men from *Princeton* down to the catwalk, and they worked aft there, fighting the fire in the vicinity of the hangar. They wanted to get into the opening so they could take hoses passed by the *Birmingham* and play them in the hangar. Another party led by Commander Murphy, the exec, played water from the flight deck on the fire in the after elevator pit, using *Birmingham*'s hoses.

It was hard going for the helping ships. *Reno* tried to come alongside to starboard to lend more hose strength. This was the wrong side for the smoke and heat were blowing back on *Reno*. She tried to pump water from the starboard quarter and then directly astern, but Captain R.C. Alexander found it tough going. *Reno* backed away, and moved in again, and then scraped against the side of the carrier so harshly that the cruiser's no. 2 40mm mount was badly damaged by the overhang, and other parts of the ship were scraped. This was no good—the wrong side—so

Reno asked permission to come around to the port quarter, and gaining it, did so. She moved in between the *Birmingham*'s stern and the *Princeton,* which made it quite crowded, and dangerous in case of trouble, and sprayed the flight deck and the hangar deck aft, helping considerably in controlling head and flame. By noon, it was decided the quarters were a little close in case of air attack, so *Reno* began to clear, suffering more damage as she did so, from the protruding sections of *Princeton*'s quarter. Now *Birmingham* swung in parallel to *Princeton* and the play of the hoses was much better. And a bit later another volunteer party came over from *Birmingham* to help—some 20 men.

Around noon, when the fire in the forward elevator had well been put out, *Princeton*'s chief engineer asked permission of Captain Buracker to go below and check out his engineering department. He could tell by now, with the diminished noise and fire, that the forward diesel engine was still running, and he hoped to be able to get some power into the ship, enough to run pumps if not to get her under way. But Captain Buracker was not yet ready to take such a chance. Wait a while, he told the chief engineer.

Now, there came another air raid from the north, with Japanese planes only five miles away. This was bound to be worrisome, because *Princeton* was standing virtually still, moving only with leeway in the sea, and to stay with her *Birmingham* was in the same exposed position. *Reno* moved away to take a position between the oncoming planes and *Princeton,* and unlimbered her anti-aircraft guns. And at the same time, around 1300, many planes were reported, and Captain Inglis, as senior officer, told *Reno* to forget the fires for a while, and take the available destroyers and keep the bogies away.

Then *Cassin Young* claimed to have heard a sound that suggested a submarine. She spent many minutes testing and tracking—but fortunately there was no submarine in the area—at least no Japanese submarines.

The *Irwin* was having her troubles in helping the carrier. At noon the electrical fires in the bridge area were put out, and it looked like they could get back to normal, and resume steering there, instead of aft. But at 1239 the ship lost power in its port engine—she had picked up some debris from the *Princeton* in the water, and it had gone into the main circulator and the condenser scoop.

But she continued her work. It was nearly over for the moment, and she was supposed to go out and screen, so the whaleboat was hoisted aboard, and *Irwin* went out to look for Japanese planes, even with only one engine.

Here is some of the talk between the ships that went on about that time:

1200 Hatchett [*Princeton*] desires her engineering crew back aboard. Thinks she can take them on bow. [*Princeton* was eager to get back to fighting the fires herself and the chief engineer had secret hopes of getting going again.]

1222 Is survivor situation well enough to assign one Cyclone to screening duty? [Captain Inglis was asking if a destroyer could be assigned to screen because of the air danger from the Japanese.]

1255 [to *Irwin*] Do you still have boats in the water? [When the answer was negative Inglis announced that he would set up anti submarine patrol because of the contact reported.]

At about noon, Captain Buracker began agitating to get his men back, and Captain Inglis agreed that if it was possible they should be returned to make the *Princeton* as self-sufficient as possible. Buracker really hoped to get the ship under control and to move to port under his own steam before the day was out. *Morrison* was asked to check the survivor situation in the water, and made one great sweep around *Princeton*, then reported that she had discovered no more men in the water and that apparently all the men who had left the carrier had been picked up. Hope was rising everywhere.

Where would *Princeton* like these men delivered? On the bow, the starboard, leeward side, if possible.

That's where they would be delivered, said *Morrison*.

Then *Morrison* was ordered to come around to the starboard side to help fight the fires there. They rose up again, so that heavy smoke pouring from the *Princeton* reduced visibility to 30 to 40 feet away. The place chosen was so close to the fire that the heat and smoke made it impossible to remain there, so she pulled up amidships and then passed over two firehoses. Now things looked like they were really going to turn out well. Captain Buracker said, ''With the *Birmingham* on our port quarter and *Morrison* amidships on the starboard side, and both of them giving us firehoses which were manned by *Princeton* personnel on both the flight and hangar decks, we made excellent progress.'' The *Birmingham*'s volunteers also helped. The fire was gradually forced aft, toward the starboard corner of the hangar, in the extreme aft. By one o'clock everyone's spirits were rising, and the Captain was sure that the fire would be put out completely in another 20 or 30 minutes.

Captain Buracker was already making plans to clear out the below decks, put the engineers back down, get up steam, and bring the ship home. *Princeton* was not very pretty, but he was certain that below and beyond the hangar deck and what had happened to the flight deck there was no serious damage. He *would* bring her home safely.

Then came trouble in two batches.

First, when *Morrison* came alongside, *Princeton* kept drifting down on her and wedged *Morrison*'s mast and forward stack between the uptakes of the carrier. The fire direction radar antenna was smashed, and *Morrison* found herself in irons, wedged against the *Princeton* and unable to move. Her stacks and mast were in danger.

The purpose was to get those engineering personnel back aboard the *Princeton*, and this was done. Hoses were sent out to *Princeton*, from the forecastle of the destroyer, amidships and aft. The rubbing grew worse—the TBS antenna was demolished and communication with other ships was lost except by voice, signal light, and semaphore. But this was all limited because of smoke and noise.

Then a tractor and a jeep fell from the flight deck of the *Princeton* onto the bridge of *Morrison*, endangering everyone there. They slipped down to the main deck, carrying away the port wing of the bridge.

There was a good deal of quiet heroism on the decks of the *Morrison*. Machinist first class V.D. Jernigan catwalked a line over to *Princeton*'s fantail, and then took two hoses that were passed to him, giving one to the First Lieutenant of the *Princeton* and manning the other one himself. He fought the fire until he was recalled to the ship. Four sailors, C.E. Savell, M. Gross, C.P. Smith, and G.J. Mitchell swam out with lines several times to rescue *Princeton* men in the water, and nearly lost their own lives as a result.

Lt. J.W. Franklin, Jr. and Lt. J.P. Simpson went to the fantail and worked to rescue men there and fight the fire, and went to the bow and directed fire-fighting parties. Lt. R.D.A. Ridge had the bridge and kept his self control when the bridge was nearly destroyed beneath him, and Lt. C.F. Conlon struggled with the communications system, using emergency rigs when TBS gear was lost.

The damage to *Morrison* continued.

The foremast was smashed, crashed, and went overboard. The port side of the bridge was nearly demolished along with the wind shield, the pelorus stand, torpedo director foundation, flag bag and lookout seat.

The port bridge bulkhead and watertight door were buckled and smashed. The flying bridge port railing was smashed, and on the main deck the port and starboard boat davits were bent.

The forward smokestack was bent at the base, and loosened, and eight feet of the after stack was sheered off on the port side of the ship. The superstructure was split and the main deck sprung. Lifelines and stanchions along the port side were torn off, and the shell plating of the ship was bent and buckled about six inches inboard. In the engine rooms machinery was forced out of place or sprung, and above decks much of the machinery and equipment was lost as the rubbing continued. Cargo lights, search lights, radio signals and other communications were smashed, bit by bit as the *Princeton* surged down on the smaller ship. Even the machine shop lathe down below was forced out of alignment by the shocking blows the ship took.

As far as her armament was concerned, *Morrison* also took a beating. The main battery director to port was crushed, and sights were demolished, the torpedo director to port was wrecked and lost and the depth charge projector firing panel was wrecked. Most of the ship's normal communications were knocked out, except for the jury rigging that could be done. Lt. Conlon rushed from this place to that one, putting men to work rigging lines and antenna so that something might be retained, but in the end he lost nearly everything.

By one o'clock the captain of *Morrison* was very definitely concerned about his ship, and a call was put in to *Irwin* to take a line and pull her away from the carrier if she would come. *Irwin* brought bow to stern of *Morrison*, and put the bow alongside *Princeton*, then passed a tow line to *Morrison*'s quarter. Swells were very difficult to maneuver and kept pushing *Irwin* into the other ships, so that she had to back away. The maneuvering was even more difficult because *Irwin* had been reduced to one engine by the fouling of her other. Now, she scraped her port side against the starboard side of *Birmingham* and destroyed the port motor whaleboat and knocked off her port anchor.

If it kept up, the navy might find itself with two badly damaged destroyers which had not even been in action against the enemy this day, except under air attack. *Princeton* was capable of wrecking their superstructure with her rolling. The lines parted, and *Morrison* seemed scarcely better off than before.

But she was better off. The lines had held long enough to move the *Morrison* in relation to the *Princeton*.

By this time, 14 streams of water were being played on

Princeton from *Birmingham*, even though the swells were also bringing the ships together, breaking lines, and causing damage to the gun mounts and superstructure of *Birmingham*. Captain Inglis was constantly manring—the lines would not hold, and it was his genius that kept the ships together so the work could continue. More volunteers went aboard *Princeton* from *Birmingham* and began to fight the fires.

Captain Inglis was very much concerned about having his ship dead in the water, and for two hours had been keeping the destroyers alert. Now, at ten minutes after one, a new danger threatened: three Japanese planes were reported to have penetrated the CAP screen. So *Reno* was told to take all the ships except *Birmingham* and patrol. But the trouble continued, and *Cassin Young* continued to have sound contacts below, which indicated a possible submarine. So Captain Inglis decided, reluctantly, that he could not remain alongside *Princeton*. He ordered the *Birmingham* crew, except for two men, to return to their ship, and the play of the water on the fires abruptly ceased. The messages told the story—the growing uncertainty about attack—the growing worry—and the events that followed:

1314 *Birmingham* from *Cassin Young*
Am investigating possible sound contact. Now bearing 185 2,000 yards from me.

1314 *Birmingham* from *Cassin Young*
Contact lost. Will attempt to regain.

1316 *Reno* from *Birmingham*
Can you see what the situation is with *Morrison* on the starboard side of *Princeton*?

1316 *Birmingham* from *Reno*
Not now. Will report later.

1319 *Birmingham* from *Cassin Young*
Have regained contact 125 1,800 yards. Am investigating.

1323 *Birmingham* from *Reno*
Morrison wedged between no. 2 and no. 3 stacks. She has just lost her foremast.

1327   *Birmingham* from *Cassin Young*
Contact lost again. Will attempt to regain.

1328   *Morrison* from *Birmingham*
We are backing clear of *Princeton* now. Stand clear.

1331   *Reno* from *Birmingham*
Birmingham will join circular screen.

1337   *Reno* from *Birmingham*
Reverse direction of rotation of screen so that *Birmingham* may unmask undamaged AA battery.

1345   *Birmingham* from *Cassin Young*
Have regained contact off and on and lost it. Classify as non-sub. Am rejoining.

    Gatling from *Irwin*
You go ahead and try to pull *Morrison* out as I have only one engine and cannot maneuver very well.

1346   *Irwin* and *Gatling Morrison* seems to clear by himself.

1352   *Birmingham* from *Reno*
Are you going to patrol by circling or shall I reverse?

    Reno from *Birmingham*
As soon as we complete this half-circle we are going to complete operations with *Princeton*. You take charge here.

Then came several messages about the impending air raid, and a final message from Captain Inglis for Admiral Sherman.

"Fire on *Princeton* now confined to after portion centered about both magazines. Prospects are very good now. *Morrison* has lost foremast. *Irwin* has one engine out of commission on account of debris in condenser. *Birmingham* has considerable superficial damage including two 5-inch mounts out of commission. *Reno* smashed one 40mm while alongside."

Then Captain Inglis called for a report on the number of *Princeton* personnel aboard the destroyers: *Reno* reported five, *Irwin* more than 500, *Gatling* some 200, and *Cassin Young* about 100.

Many things were happening at once. At 1,350 radar showed that a group of planes from the task group had intercepted a Japanese flight and that one Japanese plane was escaping southward. The CAP that was protecting *Princeton* and the group of ships around her was moved out and splashed the Japanese plane 18 miles southwest of the ships. The CAP was getting low on gasoline, down to an hour's flying time, but remained on station.

Aboard the *Princeton*, Captain Buracker and the men of the crew still on board continued to fight the fires all this while, disappointed that *Birmingham* had left at so crucial a moment with the fires nearly put out—but determined to go ahead with their own fighting.

At about this time heavy squalls descended on *Princeton* and the visibility grew very bad. Captain Buracker was pleased, however, because he hoped the water might help put out the fires. He did see one Japanese plane, but it was fired on by *Reno* and turned away without attacking. He was relieved: the gun crews of *Princeton* had abandoned ship and all the ready ammunition had been thrown over the side as a protective gesture much earlier. Visibility continued to get worse, until it was about 100 yards in all directions, and the wind reached a speed of 20 knots.

During all this time, the chief engineer had been wanting to go below and at 1330 he did so with the Captain's permission. He and one divisional officer put on rescue breathing apparatus and went forward and down to the second deck. They moved aft on the port side, finding doors too hot to touch and the smoke so thick that they could not penetrate it with a flashlight beam. They assumed there was a fire somewhere on the second deck, not far aft of Frame 57.

They went below to the third deck and farther aft to the hatch leading down to the forward engine room. The chief engineer went down the hatch and into the forward engine room to feel and look around. The heat and smoke were very severe, so that he could only remain for about a minute and a half. Battle lights were on, but he could not see anything. By holding his face and his hand battle lamp about a foot from the panel, he saw that the steam pressure was zero on all gauges and that the fire main pressure was also zero. The forward diesel was still running, though. The air temperature, he said, was about 165 degrees, and the smoke had not cleared, although the men had left the doors and hatches open when they abandoned the area that morning.

The chief engineer then staggered back above, and reported to the Captain that it would be remotely possible to get the ship under way again if the blowers could be started and the spaces cleared and cooled off, and if the people came back to the ship to man the various stations. So, by two o'clock, the men on the deck of the *Princeton* were sending semaphore signals to *Birmingham*, asking that the people needed—particularly electricians' mates—be brought back to the ship from the destroyers.

Captain Buracker was a little concerned when he learned that the chief engineer suspected a fire was burning on the second deck. The gunnery officer sent Gunner Grant and Ensign Geney down below, and they opened the remote control valves to sprinkle the forward magazines. Of course it did no good at the moment, because there was no pressure in the fire mains, but it was a precautionary measure—and one taken in great hope—the hope that the water pressure would be restored by getting up steam again.

The captain then called a conference of the officers on the *Princeton*. It was suggested that the fires were well enough under control now that it might be possible to take the ship under tow. Captain Buracker thought that if *Birmingham* would take him in tow, and *Morrison* would come alongside and fight the fires for a bit, everything would soon be resolved.

Morrison came alongside at 1453 and began playing hoses on the fire. But now it was soon realized that the fire had made considerable headway in that period when *Birmingham* was out looking for bogies. Captain Buracker said he was sure the fires could be put out, but *Morrison* could not do it and cast off two minutes later.

Then Captain Buracker suggested that *Reno* give him a tow, but a Japanese plane had hit *Reno* in the fantail in the action of recent days, and put the towing gear out of commission. So *Reno* could not do it. Then Captain Buracker suggested that *Birmingham* give him a tow and that *Reno* fight the fires while she did so. But Captain Inglis did not like that idea. *Reno* had not as good equipment for fire fighting as *Birmingham*, and besides, *Birmingham* had already suffered damage in rolling against *Princeton* that morning and *Reno* was undamaged. Why damage a second cruiser? So Inglis suggested instead that the *Birmingham* first put out *Princeton*'s fires, and then give her a tow. That suggestion was agreeable to all.

So the arrangements began. Eight electrician's mates and one fireman returned to the ship and made plans with the chief engineer to go below. *Birmingham* began approaching the port quarter, getting ready to take on her fire-fighting duties, and *Reno* stood off to become the major protective force for the group of ships involved in this mission of salvation.

Birmingham's assistant first lieutenant, Alan Reed, estimated that another hour's work would be sufficient to get those fires under control—but of course he had returned to his ship when called back to fight Japanese if necessary, and had not been observing the growth of the flames.

Captain Buracker was aware of danger—and he had been for hours. In torpedo stowage just aft of the hangar on the main deck, the crew had stowed a number of 100-pound general-purpose bombs and some fragmentation bombs, along with nine torpedo air flasks. The bombs, normally, would have been carried in the ship's magazines, but they were extras and there had seemed no other place to put them. It seemed odd, in a way, that they had not gone off in the fires that had raged around them. But since they had not gone off by this time, Captain Buracker was beginning to feel that they might not go off—that the fire had escaped them or some change had come about to protect them.

Birmingham had a good deal of difficulty in approaching *Princeton*. She made two attempts to come alongside the port quarter, but neither was satisfactory and she backed off twice. At 1515, on the third try, she approached close enough to shoot a line to the *Princeton*'s flight deck near the forward elevator. Commander Harwood, the air officer, was aft on the hangar deck with Lieutenant Bradley, the assistant first lieutenant, Lieutenant Stebbings, the First Lieutenant, Ensign Christie, and a party of 20 men. They were handling lines, and taking on firehoses—or were ready to do so.

The *Birmingham* closed with her starboard bow pointed in to *Princeton*'s port side forward of amidships. The First Lieutenant went forward in the hangar to supervise the securing of the forward lines.

Just then, all hell broke loose.

It was 1523.

CHAPTER TWELVE

The World Explodes

Captain Inglis was making his third approach to *Princeton* and the lines were across the chasm of blue water between the ships, when suddenly the world exploded.

The blast was terrible. On *Princeton*, Captain Buracker compared it to a "small volcano." The air around the two ships was filled with debris, ranging in size from dirty particles to pieces that weighed half a ton. The smoke column ascended to a height of 2,000 feet, and the flames licked at it from below. A huge part of the stern was simply knocked off and fell into the water below. Fragments showered the decks of both ships, and nearly every man left on the *Princeton* was injured, in one way or another.

An undetermined number of men were blown up or blown overboard. Commander Harwood and the whole party that had gone to the hangar to take lines and fight fires were lost in the blast.

Captain Hoskins had come to ride along with Captain Buracker as a "makee' learn"—that is, to gain experience in combat before taking over the ship and he had stayed at Captain Buracker's side all day long. Now he was down. He had been standing amidships on the port side, waiting for the lines from *Birmingham*. With the blast, Captain Buracker and others hit the deck, then they started to run forward to get behind the planes still on deck, planes that afforded some protection against whatever might come next. It was then that Captain Buracker saw that Captain Hoskins was not moving. He turned around and looked closely. Hoskins' right foot had been blown off and was hanging, suspended from his leg by a shred of skin.

Captain Buracker called for Commander Sala, the senior medical officer. Sala had been standing with them just before the explosion—but such are the ways of blasts that he now found himself on the forecastle, far forward, and he was injured. Nonetheless he came back at the Captain's cry to give first aid to Captain Hoskins.

That captain would most certainly have bled to death, except that he fell near a piece of line and used that to make a tourniquet to bind up his leg. Dr. Sala came up with sulfa powder and morphine, and a sheath knife with which he cut off the part of the foot and leg that were dangling. Only later did the doctor allow treatment of his own wounds.

As the medics moved about the ship, Captain Buracker made inspections in the hangar to see if any of the people had survived there, but only mangled bodies could be found. And yet, even after this huge explosion, in which those bombs had undoubtedly gone up—the *Princeton* below the water line was sound as ever and Captain Buracker still had many hopes that he could bring her home. He got word to *Reno*, by way of a destroyer, that he still wanted a tow. The request was forwarded to Admiral Sherman in command of the task group, and he did not immediately act on it. *Birmingham* had been further damaged by the explosion and she could not tow. Nor could *Reno*, because of the Japanese plane damage of October 14, off Formosa. Nor could the destroyers. So the matter remained in abeyance.

Captain Buracker hesitated to ask anyone else to come alongside. Three ships had been more or less seriously damaged in trying to help him this day. Also, the main magazines and the main gasoline tanks were still intact—

and they might explode. So there was no use in endangering more lives.

Considering all these facts, Captain Buracker asked *Gatling,* which was standing off the port bow, to send small boats to *Princeton* to take off the survivors. Then, if a tow ship came from the task group, the people needed could be brought back on board the ship when necessary.

No one knew what was going to happen next. Captain Buracker was hopeful, but there were rumors of fires on the second and third decks, and smoke and heat were increasing in that area. So there might be other explosions and it was time to save the men who were left.

Gatling and other destroyers sent their boats to the forecastle and Captain Hoskins was lowered into a whaleboat on a stretcher. Other wounded were helped down the Jacob's ladder by lines attached to them. Captain Buracker and Commander Murphy were the last men to leave the ship. After the Captain was sure there were no more people aboard, he followed Murphy down the ladder into the boat, and left. It was 1638. Even then, he was not satisfied and made the boat circle the *Princeton* while he looked at the ship and in the water, for possible survivors.

The ship's papers were not saved because most of them had been left on the bridge or blown up in the explosion. But it was hoped that they would go back for some, if they existed. And then the Captain arrived aboard the *Reno,* to learn what fate had in store for his ship, what decision had been made by Admiral Sherman and Admiral Mitscher.

Meanwhile, on *Birmingham,* the scene was like some nightmare in a slaughterhouse. For she had taken the full blast of the explosion across her decks, and the men were dying there in pools of blood. (The casualties were later counted at 241 dead or missing and 412 wounded, of whom more than half were seriously wounded, of a total complement of 1,243.)

The Captain, the Executive Officer, the officer of the deck, the navigator were all standing on the starboard wing of the bridge of *Birmingham*, facing *Princeton*. They were all wounded. The first lieutenant and the assistant first lieutenant were dead. The moans of the dying were horrible to hear.

The navigator and the officers of the deck were so seriously wounded they lost consciousness. The executive officer had been wounded by shrapnel, not seriously, and had also been partly deafened by the blast.

The exec asked the Captain if he was all right. The Captain did not really know, but replied that his arm was broken. He would be able to carry on, he said, and the exec was to go about his business and not worry. The Executive Officer said he thought it would be a good idea to get down to the main deck and organize first-aid parties, and investigate the damage. Captain Inglis agreed, and the executive officer went below.

Captain Inglis then ordered *Birmingham* to cast off from *Princeton*. He was afraid of more explosions. So it was done, and Inglis could then see that *Princeton* had been gutted from about the middle of the ship on aft, with her sides blown out for about 20 percent of the after part of the ship. There was also a gouge in her machinery spaces below the water line inside the outer hull. Yet he agreed with Captain Buracker that the ship's seaworthiness had not been impaired. She continued to float on an even keel.

Captain Inglis was hurt more sorely than he believed. As he backed *Birmingham* away from *Princeton*, he began to feel faint, and felt that he might lose consciousness. His first thought was for his command—he was in charge of the group as senior officer present. He decided that he must give group command to Captain Alexander of the *Reno*. He reported to *Reno* that he had many casualties on *Birmingham* and wanted *Reno* to take command. He also recommended that *Princeton* be destroyed but that was never received.

Here are the messages as they went back and forth in this critical period.

1526	*Birmingham* from *Reno*	Can you get under way?
	Reno from *Birmingham*	We are backing down. Many casualties on top side. Will try to keep under way.
1527	*Reno* from *Birmingham*	Believe we were hit by explosion on stern of *Princeton*. Give CTG 38.3 latest developments.
1532	*Reno* from *Birmingham*	Please guard all circuits except TBS. We have not been able to tell extent of damage yet.
1533	*Reno* from *Birmingham*	Try to contact *Santa Fe* tell them we need our other doctor as soon as possible.

[(*Birmingham*'s surgeon had been sent to *Santa Fe* to perform services and was not aboard at the time of the explosion.)]

	Birmingham from *Reno*	Do you want one of our doctors?
	Reno from *Birmingham*	Affirmative.
1535	*Reno* from *Birmingham*	Commanding officer is a casualty. You are in command of this group.

Now the orders began to come fast, as Captain Alexander assumed the new responsibility. First he ascertained whether or not *Birmingham* could make good speed, and was assured that she could make full speed if necessary. But *Birmingham* was busily trying to sort out the terrible state of affairs that had resulted from the blast wave smashing across the ship. It was not only the wave, but the explosion of huge chunks of debris that cleared the decks like a hail of grape shot might have in days of sail.

In the beginning, *Birmingham*'s tendency was to underestimate the casualties. The truth, that half the personnel of the ship were dead or wounded—was just too much to comprehend, paticularly in the confusion that followed the blast. So *Birmingham* reported to *Reno* that she had perhaps 100 or 150 men killed and the same number wounded—about half the truth.

Now Captain Alexander had to move in several directions simultaneously. He had to move medical people and supplies to *Birmingham*, which was obviously hard hit. He had to get the men off *Princeton* and then get a decision as to what would be done with her.

He asked the destroyers if they had boats in the water at that moment, and received replies that indicated the course of events of that fateful afternoon. *Cassin Young* had no boat in the water, and both *Irwin*'s boats had been smashed in the contact with the overhang of *Princeton* during the day.

Gatling was finally selected to get the men off *Princeton* and distribute them if necessary. *Cassin Young* was sent to search the waters around the burning carrier to see if there were any men still afloat.

Princeton, of course, was dead in the water while all this was going on, and Captain Buracker was trying desperately to maintain control of his ship—by asking for his tow. Believe it or not, when he asked, the executive officer of *Birmingham*, half out of his mind with his own troubles, agreed that *Birmingham* would tow if necessary, although it would take an hour to make a tow line. It is a measure of the failure of the communications between ships that *Reno* did not yet know the full extent of the tragedy that had hit *Birmingham*, even more than half an hour after the explosion.

The next hour was taken up with the details of taking the men off *Princeton* and moving doctors and supplies to *Birmingham*. Boats went to *Princeton* from *Gatling* and *Reno*, and the message was sent to the planes of the Combat Air Patrol to tell *Santa Fe*, off with the main body of the task group, that *Birmingham* had a real and immediate need of her senior medical officer.

The need was certainly urgent.

A few minutes after the explosion, and after he gave up command of the unit, Captain Inglis asked one of the enlisted men to bring a stool from the chart house out to the pilot house. His condition was so desperate that he was trying to hold on to consciousness, and he hoped to be able to sit high up on the stool, look out the porthole and concentrate so that he would not pass out.

He tried, and he began to get dizzy. He could feel consciousness slipping away, and called for an enlisted man. He sent for the senior unwounded officer, who turned out to be the gunnery officer, Commander Duborg. This officer had undergone an unusual experience. He had been standing on the upper bridge between two enlisted men at the time of the blast. The man on his left was killed instantly, and the man on his right was mortally wounded, but Commander Duborg was not even scratched.

Now, he came quickly to his Captain's command, and was told that he must take the con of the ship, the management of the bridge, because the Captain was not sure how much longer he could hold up.

The immediate problem was medical attention. The senior medical officer could not be expected back on the ship for several hours. The dentist had been killed in the blast. All that were left were the available and unwounded hospital corpsmen and the junior medical officer to undertake a herculean task.

At the moment, of course, all the men of *Birmingham* knew was that men were lying in their own blood all over the deck. In fact 229 men were killed outright and eight more would soon die of their injuries. There were 412 wounds ranging from skull fracture and collapsed lungs to minor burns, and half of these wounds were very serious.

Commander Winston Folk, the Executive Officer, set out from the bridge, when ordered by the Captain to see what had happened on the ship. He was completely unprepared for what he found. He was still dazed, and expected that the principal effects of the explosion would be found in the bridge area.

He found the main deck covered with dead, dying, and wounded, with those least wounded trying to help the others. Here is a part of his story:

"The communication platform was in the same condition. It is impossible, even remotely, to adequately describe the grisly scene of human fragmentation that unfolded before my eyes. I felt as if I were having a horrible nightmare and I remember wishing that I would hurry and wake up . . .

". . . there was not the slightest tendency toward panic, there was not a single case that came to my attention, directly or reportedly, where anything but praise could be given. And this with men, few of whom had ever come in close contact with violent death before, and none of whom had ever seen decks and waterways crubescent with the blood of comrades."

". . . men with legs off, with arms off, with gaping wounds in their sides, with the tops of their heads furrowed by fragments, would insist 'I'm all right. Take care of Joe over there,' or 'Don't waste morphine on me, Commander, just hit me over the head.' "

As Commander Folk made his way about the ship, he first stopped to give first aid and administer morphine to the worst cases he saw. But then his head cleared and he realized his greater responsibility, to discover how badly hurt the ship really was. What had been an exercise in discipline back in Newport News, now proved a real blessing: Folk had instituted a program of first-aid training for the men months before, never really believing that such catastrophe would strike the ship that the corpsmen could not handle it—but now he saw that the men were responding to their training, and that specialists of all kinds were turning up to give first aid to their comrades.

Men poured sulfa powder into wounds, and made tourniquets like experts. They tended the wounded with the care of real experts.

Commander Folk continued his rounds, pausing to distribute his first aid equipment. By the time he reached the second deck, all living spaces were already being filled with men treated and brought down from the bloody deck above.

Then he went back to the bridge to report to Captain Inglis, only to find, to his horror, that the Captain had turned over the con to the gunnery officer.

Captain Inglis had not been treated for his broken arm, lacerations, or burns. Now Commander Folk insisted that someone come and look at his wounds.

"Never mind me," said the Captain. "There are many in worse condition. See to them first."

But Folk insisted, and the Captain was silent. There was really nothing he could do. Folk gave his report and took command of the ship—then, as acting captain, he sent word to the junior medical officer to come and tend to Captain Inglis as soon as he was able to leave the drastic cases below.

Commander Folk began assessing the damage. The reason there were so many casualties, he reasoned, was that so many men were on deck. All the ship's anti-aircraft guns were manned, and many men from the engineering, supply, and technical divisions had come on deck to help with the work of putting out *Princeton*'s fires. Two divisions of men were working on tow lines to take the *Princeton* under tow as soon as the fire was put out.

"Shortly after I had assumed command, I was informed that *Princeton* still wanted to be towed. That seemed almost too much. With over 400 of the ship's company dead or badly wounded, and with all the remainder, including some 200 slightly to moderately wounded, not actually required on watch working their hearts out with the badly wounded, we were still faced with the prospect of having to continue to rig for towing. Yet when I consulted the acting first lieutenant, and the boatswain, the latter painfully wounded himself, their answer was 'Yes, if we have to tow we can tow.'

"I think in a sentence that expressed *Birmingham*'s spirit.

". . . So the answer was affirmative, and *Birmingham* continued to work with the tow lines among her fantail dead . . ."

Captain Inglis was now in his sea cabin, where he had gone dizzily just before Commander Folk reported to take charge of the ship. He had been stretched out on his bunk by two enlisted men who splinted his broken arm with signal flags. He lay there and listened to the talk between ships, while Commander Folk reported and gave the orders.

1645 *Reno* group this is *Reno*. Make report to *Reno* of all *Princeton* Personnel rescued, of officers and men. *Cassin Young* acknowledge.

Reno this is *Birmingham*. Believe we have but one *Princeton* enlisted man. Will inform you later. Over.

Reno this is *Gatling*. We have about 200.

1648 *Reno* this is *Birmingham*. We are in bad need of blood plasma. Can anyone supply?

From *Reno*, Wilco. Out.

1650 *Cassin Young*, *Irwin* from *Reno*. Send blood plasma to *Birmingham* as practicable. *Cassin Young*, *Irwin*, acknowledge over.

Reno this is *Irwin*. Wilco. Out.

Reno this is *Cassin Young*. Wilco. Out.

Reno this is *Cassin Young*. *Gatling* is in need of it too, over.

Reno this is *Cassin Young*. Can spare 40 units blood plasma with water without tubing. Out.

From *Reno*. Roger Wilco. Out.

From *Reno*. Send some of that to *Gatling*. Over.

1655 From *Cassin Young*. Wilco. Out.

Irwin. This is *Reno*. Can you establish guard on *Thatcher*? Over.

Reno. This is *Cassin Young*. I can send 24 units of

blood plasma complete. Stand over to *Birmingham* for transfer. Over.
1700 From *Reno*. Wilco. Out.
Birmingham this is *Cassin Young*. Affirm over.

Gatling's need for blood plasma was for the survivors of *Princeton* that she had picked up after the explosion, many of them wounded in various degrees. *Birmingham*'s need was much more serious.

The junior medical officer had a tremendous job on his hands, and he had begun organizing it within minutes after the explosion. The first step had been first aid, and luckily *Birmingham*'s men were ready for that. The medical department had to confine its activities to the seriously hurt, treatment of shock and severe hemorrhage, and application of difficult bandages. Immediately they dipped heavily into the ship's supply of blood plasma and intravenous dextrose. They would use 198 units of plasma before they were through, 500 cc of whole blood, and great quantities of dextrose and saline solution.

The second step on *Birmingham* began as soon as the medical officer could be spared from treatment of pain, hemorrhage and shock. Patients with perforated abdominal wounds were found first, and operated. Two groups of corpsmen were sent to splint fractures and treat compound fractures with sulfa powder and thick battle dressings.

Then came the third step: segregating the patients. The severe cases were taken to sick bay, and the ward room where they would have day and night care. The other cases were taken to the second and third decks of the ship. Right now they were in the second stage.

It was 1619 when Admiral Sherman received his report from the commanding officer to *Reno* telling of the damage to *Princeton* and *Birmingham* in the terrible explosion. Captain Alexander had recommended that the *Princeton* be destroyed after all personnel were removed. That recommendation was considered by Admiral Sherman, and then bucked up to Admiral Mitscher, the commander of Task Force 38.

Now, Admiral Mitscher was faced with a very tough decision. He and his chief of staff, Commodore Arleigh Burke, were considering what they might do. Captain Buracker was certain the ship could be saved even now, and she did not seem to be burning badly. But that was no longer the question. The problem was much larger: because the Japanese were now known to be launching a major naval offensive against the Americans at Leyte Gulf.

Admiral Halsey and Admiral Mitscher knew about three different Japanese forces that were moving toward Leyte. One was Nishimura's and it had been hit once early in the morning by a force, then left alone, because it was known to be moving toward the American battleships at Surigao Strait, and they were sure to take care of that group of Japanese. The smaller force of Admiral Shima was coming right behind, and did not worry anyone very much. The big force of Admiral Kurita, whose battleships and cruisers had been mauled this afternoon by the planes of Third Fleet, was now turned around and apparently headed back toward Japanese waters. But there was something new in the air.

Admiral Halsey knew at this time that the Japanese navy was making a major effort to stop the American landings at Leyte.

Just what the Japanese were up to was not quite certain. It might be an attempt to land troops, or it might be a direct attack, or both. But there was one big puzzle. Where were the Japanese carriers? The Japanese had proved at Pearl Harbor the importance of carriers in sea warfare and they had never forgotten that lesson, so there was no reason to believe they would venture out to a major battle without carriers.

The carriers, according to the best American intelligence reports—from submarines—had been located in the Inland Sea for some time. Where could they be now? There had also been indications that the Japanese had been moving their carriers around inside their own waters, probably replenishing and supplying them after the big battle of the Philippine Sea in June.

With this big an operation Halsey was certain that the Japanese would use their carriers. So the search had begun that day.

Admiral Sherman's planes had found them at 1640 and reported a force off Luzon heading south. The reports were somewhat confusing, as they always were at times of battle, but it developed that the Japanese northern group was for some reason split into two forces. There were four carriers, two battleships that had been half converted to carriers, three cruisers, and eight destroyers, a number of escort vessels smaller than destroyers, and two oilers.

Admiral Halsey decided that the northern force might have as many as 24 ships, and he decided that since the carriers were there the northern force remained the greatest threat to the Americans. He decided, then, too, that he was going to move north after that force.

Admiral Mitscher learned that Admiral Halsey was going to take Third Fleet and move north fast with it, he knew what he had to do. Sadly, Chief of Staff Burke made the decision which was ratified by his chief and passed down the line.

Princeton was to be destroyed.

CHAPTER THIRTEEN

The Death of the Princeton

If Commodore Burke had been given a glimpse into the future, he would never have recommended to Admiral Mitscher that *Princeton* be destroyed. Instead, he would have beached her. But beaching was a difficult operation, involving several ships and many men, and *Princeton* that day had already tried the patience of the fleet sorely with her antics. She had severely damaged three ships and caused the deaths of hundreds of men.

So the decision was made, and passed down the fleet line of command.

By the time that Captain Alexander received the message from task group, Captain Buracker was aboard, and he listened to the death sentence for his command. He reasoned that it must come, because the fires were still burning on *Princeton* and night was falling. She would blaze like a beacon, leading the enemy to the fleet. And the fleet only 125 miles away from Manila and its circle of airfields—Japanese airfields. Also, he learned about the presence of this new Japanese force in the north, and he accepted all these reasons and knew that he must lose his ship.

Just then, came a TBS from *Birmingham*.

1701. From *Birmingham*, *Reno*, this is *Birmingham*.

Can you tell us whether you want us to tow *Princeton?* Over.

Four minutes later came the second message, urgently.

1705. *Reno.* This is *Birmingham.* Can you tell us whether you want us to tow *Princeton?* Over.

From *Reno.* Roger. Wait. Out.

Then, a minute later . . .

1706. *Irwin* this is *Reno.* Torpedo and destroy *Princeton.* Over.

From *Irwin.* Roger. Out.

From *Reno.* Torpedo and use gunfire if necessary.

From *Irwin.* Wilco.

1706. *Birmingham* this is *Reno.* You received my transmission to *Irwin*, did you not?

Reno, this is *Birmingham.* Roger. Out.

Captain Alexander was in a hurry now. He had his orders, to get the *Princeton* sunk and to join up with the task group. He could sense that the fleet was getting to move.

A few minutes later he sent another message.

1711. *Irwin*, this is *Reno.* Expedite. Over.

1712. *Reno* this is *Irwin.* Roger. Out.

While he waited, Captain Alexander was busy with housekeeping chores relative to his little fleet. He moved *Cassin Young* and *Birmingham* closer in for transmission purposes. Then he called for a report on damage to ships and people.

1718. *Reno* group from *Reno.* Expedite making survivor report and own damage. *Birmingham* and *Cassin Young.* Wilco. Out.

These were the ships with the sorely hurt men aboard.

At 1724 *Birmingham* was able to give a preliminary, but much underestimated report of survivors and injured.

Reno from *Birmingham.* We are ready to proceed. Engineering plant is in perfect condition. Two five-inch mounts out. 150 to 300 badly wounded. Over.

1725. From *Reno.* Roger. Out.

1727. From *Birmingham.* One forty and four twenties

knocked out. 150 badly wounded. 75 to 100 killed. Two five-inch mounts knocked out. Top side is pretty well battered up. Over.

It was also a time to begin rounding up equipment, and to prepare to move fast.

1728. *Irwin* from *Morrison*. Do you have our boat?

1729. *Reno* to *Cassin Young*. What is your present intention?

1730. *Cassin Young*. I am going to join up with *Reno*.

There was a moment—so common in warfare—when a bogie was reported at 260 degrees but it turned out to be a false alarm so the group continued its activity.

At 1730 *Gatling* announced she had 191 survivors of *Princeton* aboard, and was getting ready to give a breakdown of their condition.

Aboard the *Birmingham*, Commander Folk reported the damage to Captain Inglis, who lay dizzily on his bunk. The ship's upper works above the main deck were peppered and perforated almost unbelievably. Most of the delicate instruments associated with fire control and radar and communication were at least temporarily out of commission due to blast damage or the severing of electric wires or by flying debris. But there was no damage below the water line except to the No. 1 propeller shaft, which had been damaged by debris from the *Princeton*. One compartment had been ruptured below the waterline, but that was not serious and had been stopped. The really serious damage was to the men themselves, and this was the decimation of half the crew as an effective fighting unit.

From the brave little destroyers came the word of the fate of the men of *Princeton*, and it was encouraging to Captain Buracker when he learned. It had been difficult to keep up with his crew, because some casualties had been taken off in the morning, men had left the ship all day long and gone into the water, and then the remainder had been saved by the destroyers after the explosion.

But actually, because of those destroyers, *Princeton*

suffered fewer than ten percent casualties to her crew. She had one dead officer and six enlisted men, nine mission officers and 92 enlisted men (including those who obviously perished in the explosion in the hangar) and 191 wounded. It was almost unbelievable.

Irwin had the unpleasant job of the day—the destruction of a brave and once handsome ship, a companion in arms with which she fought many battles and sailed many seas. It was not an easy job, but commander D.B. Miller set about it with all his skill. Unfortunately, after the day's pounding against the side of *Princeton,* skill was not all that was required.

Obeying his orders, the captain closed on *Princeton* at 1700, moving in to 2,000 to 2,500 yards from the ship. Torpedo officer, Ensign G.M. Stout, got ready to fire.

He fired one. It ran hot enough, but curved to the left, and hit *Princeton* forward on the bow, inflicting very little damage.

The second torpedo ran hot, straight, and normal—except that it passed astern of the *Princeton* and never did explode.

The third torpedo ran erratically, broaching water several times and circling to the left.

The fourth torpedo ran hot, but curved to the left and passed ahead of the *Princeton.* So did the fifth.

The sixth torpedo ran erratically, broached, and seemed to be coming back to hit the ship. Captain Miller took evasive action.

What a strain on everyone! Obviously during the day's pounding against the side of the carrier, the destroyer had damaged her torpedo control mechanisms. During the firing, Ensign Stout noted excessive whip of the tube mount, and there may have been other troubles: the torpedoes might even have been damaged during the day by the pounding the little ship had taken.

By 1733 Captain Alexander was getting nervous and irritated. He sent a message:

Irwin from *Reno*. Have you made any torpedo hits? Over.

Reno from *Irwin*. Have made one hit. Director is out of commission. Over.

Irwin, this is *Reno*. *Reno* will fire broadside of torpedoes. Stand clear when she comes in. Over.

Meanwhile, *Irwin* had been trying her best. She had missed with all but one torpedo, but she opened fire with her guns, and started a severe fire in the forecastle and among the parked planes on the forward end of the flight deck—planes that had so far withstood every damage of the ship that day. And she restarted the fire in the hangar. From the ships nearby, in the growing dusk, the men could see the fires blazing up, the pyre of their own ship, so to speak.

Captain Alexander moved in, and this time there was no mistake. At 1746 he fired a torpedo and at 1747 he fired another, and in three minutes they hit. The first hit in the vicinity of the forward gasoline tanks, and main magazines, and the second hit just afterward. They were set at 12 feet where they were calculated to do the most damage.

Wham! They did.

The torpedoes hit and the magazines went up and flames shot up from the carrier five hundred feet in the air, followed by smoke to thousands of feet, and the earsplitting explosion made its way across the water. Eighty thousand gallons of aviation gasoline had gone up, along with bombs and torpedoes and thousands of rounds of ammunition.

So the *Princeton*, brave and mighty ship, went to her grave deep in the Philippine Sea. In forty-five seconds she completely disintegrated and all that was left of her was fire on the water. Her burial place was 15 degrees 12 minutes North, 123 degrees 36 minutes East.

EPILOGUE

Given the tactical situation that developed, the wisdom of scuttling *Princeton* was proved that very night, for Third Fleet did indeed move out to the north chasing Admiral Ozawa's northern Japanese force. Nothing else but beaching could have been done with the carrier, and at the moment, no one knew when they might return, or what might happen in these waters. Almost certainly, had she been beached, she would have been a prime target for the Japanese air force—carriers always were.

But she was avenged, no question about that. When Admiral Halsey moved north against Ozawa, and Admiral Kurita of the center force turned about and moved to close the pincers on Leyte Gulf, there were three battles to be fought—one at Surigao Strait, one off Samar and one off Cape Engano. And then, when the Japanese were defeated in all three, there was the question of sending American planes after the remnants. All four Japanese carriers were sunk, so was the mighty battleship *Musashi* and so were the battleships *Yamashiro* and *Fuso*. So were sunk eight cruisers and nearly a score of destroyers. The Americans lost *Princeton*, the most important ship hurt in the battle, two escort carriers, and a handful of destroyers and escorts. It was in every way a stunning American victory, and the revenge for *Princeton* was great.

But that night, with these battles yet to come, as *Princeton* dissolved in a puddle of flame on the darkening water, Captain Buracker aboard the *Reno* could comfort himself with the fact that *Princeton* in her short life had served the United States Navy well. She had knocked down—or her pilots had—185 Japanese planes with a loss of only seven of her own pilots. She had participated in some of the most important and decisive actions of the war. She had done a good job.

Reno gathered her "small boys," or destroyers, around herself and *Birmingham*, and learned that *Birmingham* could make full speed, so she set a course and a speed of 20 knots to rejoin the task group, and at 1756, turned away from the burning water that was *Princeton*'s grave and headed toward Admiral Sherman, duty completed.

They were counting noses for the *Princeton*'s crew that evening. *Irwin* had 50 officers and 586 men aboard by that time; *Gatling* had 13 officers and 178 men—so the men were being accounted for.

Birmingham took station 1,500 yards astern of *Reno*, and they moved on through the evening. There was a problem, though. *Birmingham*'s shaft damage made it necessary for her to stop and shut down one screw, and this would take a little time. This was accomplished by 1930, and they went on. Nine minutes later they secured from General Quarters—the dangers of the day were over, and the dangers of the night had not yet begun.

The reports came in, more thoroughly this time, on the saving of the *Princeton* crew, and on the dead and wounded on *Birmingham*, and by 2032 the *Reno* group was basically dissolved, with the ships told to proceed immediately to join the task group. At 2040 *Birmingham* issued her comprehensive report, noting that 200 of its wounded required immediate hospitalization, and that the No. 1 screw was damaged and locked to prevent vibration. Obviously, *Birmingham* was not a very good candidate for the long, hard, fast run up north to fight the Japanese that night.

The evening messages began piling in. Admiral Mitscher

congratulated Admiral Sherman and his men for the way they had handled themselves that day, and said he was proud to ride with them. They talked about what should be done with the cripples. Admiral Sherman wanted to send *Birmingham* and one other ship back to base and get medical supplies from oilers. But he was not sure that was the right course. Admiral Mitscher settled it: he ordered *Birmingham* detached along with *Irwin* and *Morrison,* all of them damaged to some degree. They would form a unit and proceed to Ulithi for hospitalization and repair of the ships. And then *Gatling* was added to the group. Because her engineering plant was in bad shape, she carried many *Princeton* survivors, and neither *Morrison* nor *Irwin* had any radar left.

From early in the evening *Birmingham* had the services of one of *Reno*'s doctors, and then at 2232 that night, the destroyer *Cotten* brought up her own senior medical officer, who had gone away (it seemed so long ago) to operate on the senior medical officer at *Santa Fe.*

Birmingham got her own doctor back that night, and kept *Reno*'s doctor as well, for he was badly needed there. So the ships pulled away in formation, taking care to keep close to *Birmingham* whose radio was down and who had to rely on TBS for transmission of messages. Thus the long day ended, and the ships steamed peacefully through a night as calm as though there were no war at all.

Captain Inglis finally was treated for his wounds about nine o'clock that night and along with the other wounded he was transferred to the hospital ship *Samaritan* when they reached Ulithi three days later. He was treated there, the most serious cases were taken off, and he went back to the West Coast in *Birmingham,* arriving on November 22.

Captain Buracker went back to the United States, too, and was very pleased to learn that the Secretary of the Navy had decided to name one of the new large carriers, now being built, in honor of the fighting ship that had gone down so tragically.

Captain Hoskins went into the hospital. His amputated

leg was treated and eventually he was restored to duty with an artificial foot—although there was some argument in the Navy Department that he really ought to accept being invalided out of the service.

The other captains went on to distinguished service. Captain Buracker won the Navy Cross and the Purple Heart for his actions and his injuries. He went back to duty as senior navy air instructor at the Army-Navy staff college in Washington, and then continued in training work until he retired in 1947 as a Rear Admiral.

Captain Inglis' career was equally distinguished. He won the Navy Cross for rescue work on the *Princeton* and the Purple Heart for his injuries. He was out of action until 1945 when he became deputy of the Office of Naval Intelligence, and later chief of Naval Intelligence. He retired as a Vice Admiral.

In spite of the difficulties of Captain Hoskins' situation (with the aid of Admiral Nimitz and others some of the practices of the Navy were changed) he received command of a *Princeton*. It was not CVL 23, of course, but the new, bigger *Princeton* that became the pride of the fleet. And yet, no man who ever served aboard the light carrier *Princeton* would have changed the duty. She was a heroic ship. She died a lady.

FROM PERSONAL JOURNALS TO BLACKLY HUMOROUS ACCOUNTS

VIETNAM

DISPATCHES, Michael Herr
01976-0/$3.95 US/$5.50 Can
"I believe it may be the best personal journal about war, any war, that any writer has ever accomplished."
—Robert Stone, *Chicago Tribune*

A WORLD OF HURT, Bo Hathaway
69567-7/$3.50 US/$4.50 Can
"War through the eyes of two young soldiers...a painful experience, and an ultimately exhilarating one."
—*Philadelphia Inquirer*

NO BUGLES, NO DRUMS, Charles Durden
69260-0/$3.50 US/$4.50 Can
"The funniest, ghastliest military scenes put to paper since Joseph Heller wrote *Catch-22*"
—*Newsweek*

AMERICAN BOYS, Steven Phillip Smith
67934-5/$3.95 US/$5.75 Can
"The best novel I've come across on the war in Vietnam"
—Norman Mailer

COOKS AND BAKERS, Robert A. Anderson
79590-6/$2.95
"A tough-minded unblinking report from hell"
—*Penthouse*

WORLD WAR II
Edwin P. Hoyt

BOWFIN   **69817-X/$3.50 US/$4.95 Can**

An action-packed drama of submarine-chasing destroyers.

THE MEN OF THE GAMBIER BAY   **55806-8/$3.50 US/$4.75 Can**

Based on actual logs and interviews with surviving crew members, of the only U.S. aircraft carrier to be sunk by naval gunfire in World War II.

STORM OVER THE GILBERTS: **63651-4/$3.50 US/$4.50 Can**
War in the Central Pacific: 1943

The dramatic reconstruction of the bloody battle over the Japanese-held Gilbert Islands.

TO THE MARIANAS: **65839-9/$3.50 US/$4.95 Can**
War in the Central Pacific: 1944

The Allies push toward Tokyo in America's first great amphibious operation of World War II.

CLOSING THE CIRCLE: **67983-8/$3.50 US/$4.95 Can**
War in the Pacific: 1945

A behind-the-scenes look at the military and political moves drawn from official American and Japanese sources.

McCAMPBELL'S HEROES   **68841-7/$3.95 US/$5.75 Can**

A stirring account of the daring fighter pilots, led by Captain David McCampbell, of Air Group Fifteen.

THE SEA WOLVES   **75249-2/$3.50 US/$4.95 Can**

The true story of Hitler's dreaded U-boats of WW II and the allied forces that fought to stop them.

THE CARRIER WAR   **75360-X/$3.50 US/$4.50 Can**

The exciting account of the air and sea battles that defeated Japan in the Pacific.

ALL BOOKS ILLUSTRATED
WITH MAPS AND ACTION PHOTOGRAPHS